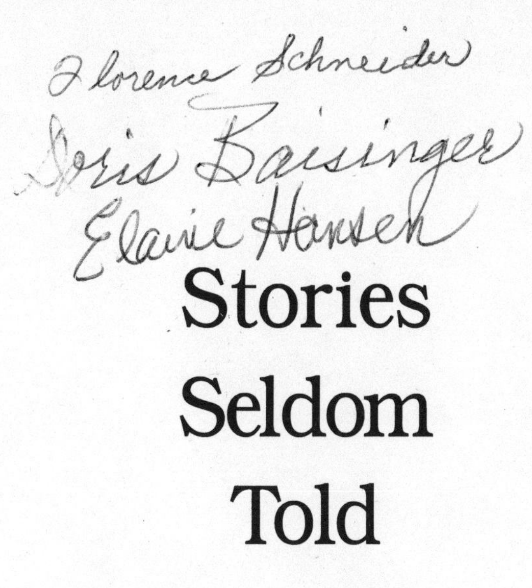

Stories Seldom Told

Biblical Stories
Retold for
Children & Adults

Lois Miriam Wilson

Stories Seldom Told

Biblical Stories Retold for Children & Adults

Northstone

Editing: Jim Taylor
Consulting art director: Robert MacDonald
Cover design: Lois Huey-Heck

Northstone Publishing Inc. is an employee-owned company, committed to caring for the environment and all creation. Northstone Publishing recycles, reuses and composts, and encourages readers to do the same. Resources are printed on recycled paper and more environmentally friendly groundwood papers (newsprint), whenever possible. The trees used are replaced through donations to the Scoutrees for Canada Program. Ten percent of all profit is donated to charitable organizations.

Canadian Cataloguing in Publication Data

Wilson, Lois, 1927–
Stories Seldom Told

Includes bibliographical references.
ISBN 1-896836-03-8
1. Bible stories, English. 2. Women in the Bible. I. Title.
BS575.W547 1997 220.9'505 C96-910889-3

Published by
Northstone Publishing Inc.

Printed in Canada by Friesens Printing

Printing 10 9 8 7 6 5 4 3 2 1

"Maybe Granddad did me a favor. We can get along pretty well without all that religious baggage, don't you think?"

"A favor? He did you a favor? It's *good* that you turned away from that rich world of stories that could guide you on a journey towards freedom? No. It wasn't a favor."

Joy Kogawa
from *The Rain Ascends*
(Alfred A. Knopf, 1995, p. 185)

Dedication

To those who are sustained and enlivened
by this "rich world of stories"
and to those who tell them to children.

Table of Contents

Women of the early church

Women crossing boundaries

Strong women

Women of the Hebrew Scriptures

Women of the Greek Scriptures

Introduction

A former kindergarten teacher told me this story.

As Good Friday was approaching, she asked her class, "What happened on Good Friday?"

The answer came: "Jesus was killed."

She was quite pleased about that response, and decided to probe further: "Does anyone know why he was killed?"

Another child put up her hand. "Because he ate the poisoned apple."

Some children think Noah's Ark is a fairy tale. They know more about Big Bird than about Rebekah or Rachel, or Mary or Prisca. I hope this book can help to remedy that lack of knowledge.

Children will need to know these stories, should they ever decide to become Christian. It will be like having furniture to move into the new house.

Stories seldom told

These stories are seldom told because so many of them are laced with violence. Parents don't voluntarily tell stories of terror to their children; many avoid such stories entirely because they seem to contradict Christian principles of love. Preachers, similarly, generally avoid preaching on these troublesome texts. And there are many women who have flat out rejected the church because of these tales.

Then why were they entered into the biblical text? What possible redeeming qualities do they have? Why do Christians intone in their liturgies, "This is the Word of God," when the story itself seems to indicate the opposite?

So why tell them?

Some of the stories are there because the biblical text reflects human life, both good and bad. Today, stories of rape, incest, physical violence, and betrayal are accepted as part of human existence. But acknowledging these stories is not to condone these actions. Children know this.

So some of these stories are told with the hope that their actions may never be repeated again in human history (for example, the story of Jephthah's daughter). Some of them come out of a particular historical time, in a cultural setting that legitimized violence as an instrument of war and conquest. Children know this happens today, also.

One reason for retelling these stories is to help us discover where the experience of our faith community intersects with the biblical story.

Today, women and children in many parts of the world who are victims of violence can help us understand better the struggles in the biblical stories. The characters they portray, while different from us, are very like us. They speak of who we are as a people of God. Their story, and ours, is one of deceit, of trickery, of struggle, of joy, shame, triumph, despair, and love.

Different lenses needed

Some swear the moon is round. Others call it a crescent. How you see it depends on your vantage point. What's often assumed to be a "universal" truth is, in fact, partial.

It is now widely acknowledged that the biblical text is a patriarchal document. The stories were written by men, about men, and have been interpreted for centuries by men. Many of them came out of a bias that didn't bother to tell the story from the woman's perspective, yet they have been interpreted as if they convey universal truths.

In our time, women have begun to read, tell, and interpret those same stories through the lens of women's struggles for justice and wholeness. They have begun to use a different lens.

The recorded biblical stories remain the basis for these stories. They are rooted in the Judaic-Christian knowledge of a God who sets people free and who requires justice and mercy, both in the personal and in the public socio-economic political sphere.

I have chosen, however, to retell these stories in new ways, ways that are informed by women's contemporary struggles and perspectives.

Many of these stories have never been singled out as central to the story of salvation. I have chosen them precisely because they are stories of women on the margins. By my reading of the gospel, those on the margins are always central to the story of salvation. Jesus' attention was persistently captured by the widow, the orphan, the stranger, the poor.

Informed by feminist theologians

Some of us act as if there have been no theological discoveries or fresh ideas, theologically speaking, in the past 50 years. We are content to repeat traditional interpretations of biblical stories without questioning those interpretations in the light of contemporary scholarship. We have not matured in our religious thinking as we have, for instance, in our scientific thinking.

This book attempts to introduce readers to some of the concepts, interpretations, and theology of internationally respected feminist theologians. I have attempted to popularize their work, which continues to provoke and stimulate me. The resource books that I have included with the "Background" sections for each story are available through denominational bookstores or through theological libraries, should you choose to do some interesting reading for your own nurture.

What these stories are not

These stories are not morality tales. After telling one of the stories from *Miriam, Mary, and Me* in a church service, a ten-year-old boy asked me, "What's the moral of the story?" I said it was like a good joke – if I had to explain the moral, the point was gone.

They are not just about "good" people. Church schools get a bad name when their teachers emphasize only stories of "good" people. That does not reflects life as it is. Conversely, stories of superwomen or supermen, heroines or heroes who act entirely on their own, are equally unhelpful.

Neither of these approaches reflects who we, a small part of the people of God, are to be today.

These stories are not based on the lectionary in use in most churches today, because it too is an arbitrary ordering of biblical passages by predominantly male theologians. Churches who adhere strictly to the lectionary will never read publicly many of the stories about women told in this book.

Parental guidance required

It is difficult to designate a story as appropriate for a particular age group, or for a particular occasion. So parental guidance and discretion are required. You know the children to whom you tell these stories. Use your judgment.

I for one do not want to reinforce the complicity of the churches in deleting or ignoring these stories of violence, particularly for children. To "protect" children that way is to deny them an awareness that their faith has struggled against violence. They will not thank us when they mature and come to realize that we have skipped half the historical record.

How then, do we highlight women's stories from Scripture, facing up to the reality of the violence which is undoubtedly there, without violating the stories themselves by de-emphasizing their intrinsic violence and turning them into harmless morality lessons? This book attempts to address that question.

For that reason, I have included stories of trickery and violence in this book – not to commend them, but to reflect life as it really was and is.

Who wrote these stories?

I am responsible for the final text of most of the stories. But it was not one individual's efforts that produced them. Some come from Hebrew folk tales. One comes from the United Kingdom.

And once a month, in the winter of 1995–96, a lively group of women of the "Spirit Rising" group of St. James Bond United Church congregation in Toronto contributed their life experiences, the intersections of their stories with the story, their insights and questions, to the drafts.

What becomes exciting in this process is that we women begin to see ourselves collectively as storytellers. Stories should always be told in groups. In circles. With lots of laughter. And, sometimes, with tears.

Thanks and acknowledgments

Thanks to those who participated in developing the theological approaches to the stories; to those who actually penned stories and permitted me to make use of them; to children and grandchildren who listened to these stories and contributed new shades of meaning from their own understanding; to Jim Taylor, my editor; and to my husband Roy, who has endured countless hours of my exit to the computer.

An invitation

To call the church to conversion and repentance requires the participation of many people. To effect a change in direction, I invite your participation as a storyteller.

There are more stories to be written.

Some come from the Bible, some from our own lives. All this book attempts is to point you, the reader, in a particular direction. It is a beginning only. Try your hand, make your own exploration, tell your own story, and see how it intersects with the biblical story.

The method is clear. Demolish stereotypes of biblical women. Expose and uncover the roles of women and the way they functioned within a highly patriarchal society. Write stories about independent women that will strengthen the image of women in children's eyes. Avail yourself of theological scholarship growing out of women's struggles, worldwide.

Be aware of the difficulties. We are probably no wiser than the original writers. Women are not blameless or perfect, nor should they be made to appear so. Remember that the Bible speaks out of a world of which we are mainly ignorant. Do not read 20th century assumptions about the role of women back into the text. Reinforce the continuity of Scripture and its common themes by honoring the Hebrew as well as the Greek scriptures – the "Old" as well as the "New" Testaments.

And enjoy!

– Lois Miriam Wilson

Jesus and women

The adulterous woman

John 7:53–8:11

Invited to new life

This story of the woman "taken in adultery" by the scribes and Pharisees is, in most editions of the New Testament, printed in the text as John 7:53–8:11. Not until the 3rd century CE did this story find its way into the official canon. Even today, some versions of the Bible print it as an addition to the text, or as a subtext. The early church thought that Jesus' words of forgiveness to a woman charged with adultery were at odds with the church's discipline of penance. Augustine feared that the text could "make women immune to punishment for their sins." The difficulty that this story had in being accepted into the official scriptures reflects the difficulty that the church found in harmonizing it with the male orientation dominant at the time.

You will have to read the story before you read the rest of this introduction, or nothing will make sense!

Traditional interpretation focuses exclusively on the woman and on her sexual behavior as "sin." This interpretation can be traced back to Augustine, the most influential theologian of his time, who emphasized that the text made Jesus the embodiment of grace and the woman the embodiment of sin. Yet the text does not isolate the woman's sin, nor does Jesus single out the woman as "sinner." Moreover there is not a word about the adulterous man. Under the law, he should also have been apprehended and punished.

The law was clear about adultery: capital punishment for both men and women (Leviticus 20:10 and Deuteronomy 22:22). The same punishment applied to idolatry. Both offenses were seen as harming the honor and integrity of the community's life.

In this incident, though, the patriarchal law is being misused against a woman.

Rejecting the strong invitation to join in the stoning (verse 5), Jesus acts with civil courage. It is not likely that he repudiated the scripture which called for the execution of adulterous women. But he knew that was only half the law (Leviticus 20:10). Jesus was an interpreter of scriptural tradition, not one who rejected tradition outright. He takes sides with the afflicted and debased woman. He – and those who told and retold this story until it was accepted into the official canon of scripture – thought of adultery as a sin, but no longer as a capital crime. Such a judgment challenged patriarchy at one of its crucial points – power over women's sexuality.

The story has three scenes.

The first scene shows the Pharisees

and scribes bringing the woman "caught in adultery" – complete with the required two witnesses – to Jesus to force him to judge her. But they quoted only half the law: "In the law, Moses commanded us to stone such women. Now what do you say?" (8:5). They hoped to trap him in an open-and-shut case.

Scene two begins in 8:6b when Jesus bends down and writes on the ground with his finger. He knew that guilt cannot be assigned according to one's sex. We don't know what he wrote. Perhaps he just doodled in the dust to stall for time. Perhaps he wrote something that indicated his unwillingness to spring the trap that has been set for him. Perhaps he was putting the "sins" of the woman on the same level as the trespasses of the men – be they theft, fraud, adultery, or anything else. Interpretations that focus entirely on the woman and on sexual behavior as sin have not read the text carefully. The text does not isolate the woman's sin.

In the Bible, often the most important part is not written down, but is left out. Thus in the Apostle's Creed, we jump from "born to the Virgin Mary" to "suffered under Pontius Pilate." Think of all that's left out! Similarly, in this passage, what Jesus wrote is missing, but important. When they continue to press him, he stands and addresses them.

The third scene starts at 8:8 when Jesus bends down and writes on the ground again. He seems to be using the action almost as a way of not confronting the woman's accusers eye to eye. Intentional or not, it gives them the opportunity to slink away, reflecting the order of succession in stoning rituals – elders first! The crowd leaves. Jesus stands up again and speaks to the woman twice. "Has no one condemned you?" And then, "Go and sin no more."

Gail O'Day, in the *Women's Bible Commentary,* notes that Jesus focuses equally on the scribes and Pharisees and the woman. He treats the woman as their equal. He speaks to both sets of characters about sin. He enjoins the Pharisees, "Let anyone among you who is without sin cast the first stone," implying that the men before him are guilty of plenty of sins, whether or not those sins include adultery. He then says to the woman (but not to the men) "Neither do I condemn you. Go and sin no more" – a clear direction for the way she could live the future.

It's an astonishing judgment in the light of the Jewish law, in which Jesus was doubtless well versed – a law that applied equally to both men and women. He refused to sanction punishment, stoning, community rejection, public shaming in order to motivate people to sin no more.

Interpretations that focus entirely on the woman and sexual behavior as sin fail to consider the text carefully. The text does not isolate the woman's sin. Rather all of them – scribes, Pharisees, and the woman – are invited by Jesus to put their old ways behind them, and to accept grace and mercy and a new way of living.

Christians must guard against anti-Semitism in telling this story. It is easy to make the scribes and Pharisees (all Jews) the bad guys and the woman the victim. The patriarchal culture of the day viewed women not only as the property of men but subject to their authority. Adultery by a woman was thought of as an injury to the husband's property, his right of sole possession of his wife's sexuality. It was a violation of both the authority and the property rights of the male; hence the harsh calls for vengeance. Israel understood sexual offenses as religious offenses. They were not private matters, but a vital concern to the whole community.

Nevertheless, it is a mistake to think of a complete discontinuity between the Hebrew Scriptures (the "Old Testament") and the Greek scriptures (the "New Testament"). Feminist scholarship has pointed to the fact that there were many openings and an emerging degree of freedom for women at the time of Jesus. American theologian Bernadette Brooten has concluded that women interacted with Jesus because they were already questioning the confines of their culture, and they sensed in him someone who supported and strengthened their desire for liberation.

Even in this story, Jesus was able to persuade a number of Jewish men not to apply a vindictive law against an adulterous woman. Jesus himself was a Jew. His attitude to women as depicted in this story does not represent a radical discontinuity with his Jewish roots but rather the possibility of renewal within Judaism.

For further reading

Bird, Phyllis. "Images of Women in the Old Testament" in *Religion and Sexism,* ed. Rosemary Radford Ruether. Simon and Schuster, NY, 1974.

Brooten, Bernadette. *Women Leaders in the Ancient Synagogue*. Scholars Press, Chico, CA, 1982

von Kellenbach, Katharina. *Anti-Judaism in Feminist Writings*. The American Academy of Religion, Scholars Press, Atlanta, GA, 1994.

Newsom, Carol A. and Sharon H. Ringe, eds. *The Women's Bible Commentary*. Westminster/John Knox, Louisville, 1992.

Schottroff, Luise. *Lydia's Impatient Sisters: A Feminist Social History of Early Christianity*. Westminster/John Knox, Louisville, 1995, pp. 180 ff.

Invited to new life

There once was a woman
Of great sin accused.
But those throwing stones
Were ashamed to abuse.

I was at the temple listening to Jesus teaching. Suddenly some older men burst through the crowds. They brought a woman, and flung her on the ground in front of Jesus. They pushed her so hard she landed on her hands and knees. But they wouldn't leave her there. They grabbed her, and made her stand up again in the middle of a circle of doctors of the law.

"Master," they said, "this woman was caught having sex with a man who is not her husband." They pointed fingers at her. The crowds rumbled. The noise got louder.

"The law says that she should be stoned to death," the leaders chanted above the noise of the crowd. But it was only half the law.

"Stoned to death! Stoned to death!" The crowds picked up the chant.

"And what do you say about it?" the leaders jeered at Jesus.

"Shame! Shame!" hissed the crowd.

"Guilty! Guilty!" grumbled the crowd.

"Disgraceful! Disgraceful!" shouted the crowd.

"Stone her! Stone her!" yelled the crowd.

Wow! Jesus knew they were trying to trap him. If he agreed with them about the law, then they would stone the woman. But he knew it was only half the law.

But if he disagreed, they would accuse him of false teaching. And they would probably incite the crowd to lynch him, for interpreting the law of Moses differently from them.

It was a trap. And they were using the woman as bait.

Instead of answering them, Jesus bent down and wrote with his finger in the dust.

The leaders kept on chanting: "The law says she should be stoned to death." But it was only half the law.

"Stoned to death! Stoned to death!" The crowds picked up the chant.

"And what do you say about it?" jeered the leaders.

"Shame! Shame!" hissed the crowd.

"Guilty! Guilty!" grumbled the crowd.

"Disgraceful! Disgraceful!" shouted the crowd.

"Stone her! Stone her!" yelled the crowd.

Finally, Jesus stopped writing in the dust. He stood up straight. He looked them straight in the eye, and he said: "The one of you who is without sin may throw the first stone."

Wow! That stopped them in their tracks. They all knew that no one was without sin. Many of them had stoned women to death in the past. The crowd had done so too, even though it was only half the law. They all knew that the full law required **both** the man **and** the woman to be stoned to death. But they thought it was more shameful for a woman to have sex with a man who was not her husband, than for a man to have sex with a woman who was not his wife.

Each of them knew he was not without fault in his own life.

The leaders stopped chanting, "The law says she should be stoned to death." Even if it was only half the law.

The crowd stopped roaring, "Stoned to death! Stoned to death!"

The leaders stopped jeering, "What do you say about it?"

The crowd stopped hissing, "Shame! Shame!"

They didn't grumble, "Guilty! Guilty!"

They didn't shout, "Disgraceful! Disgraceful!"

They didn't yell, "Stone her! Stone her!"

Instead, their feet began to shuffle.

Their faces became red.

They didn't look at each other. They looked at the ground, or the buildings, or the sky.

Not one of them looked at Jesus. They were so ashamed.

And not one of them threw a stone.

Wow! Once again, Jesus bent and wrote on the ground. Some of the feet stopped shuffling, so they could see what he wrote. Some of the faces lost their redness, as they paid attention. Some of the men looked at each other and nodded, as they got the message.

One by one some of the doctors of the law slunk away, feeling ashamed. But a few of the others left in groups of three or four, eagerly talking. They had understood Jesus' invitation to a new way of life.

Jesus was left alone with the woman, still standing there. Except for me, of course. I stuck around to listen.

Jesus looked around. He saw no one left but the woman. And me.

He said to the woman, "What happened to those who accused you? Has no one thrown a stone at you?"

"No one, sir," she replied.

He didn't ask her how her husband would feel about all this. Instead, he stood up and said, "Neither do I condemn you. You may go as a free woman. Do not repeat your sin."

Wow! That stopped her in her tracks. She hadn't expected that. She looked at Jesus, and then looked away from him. She covered her face with her hands. I thought I heard her sob. I could tell she wasn't sure how to respond. I bet it's not often she has heard such words of mercy. What a chance for a new life!

Then I saw her slowly stand up straight. She looked Jesus fully in the face. And then, with her shoulders firm and with great dignity, she left the temple courtyard. On her own.

Sister Jessica

Matthew 13:56 and Mark 6:3

Why'd he have to be my brother?

Two gospels record that Jesus had at least two sisters, but neither elaborates on that point. What follows is an imaginative story about Jesus, told from the perspective of one of his younger sisters. Be sure that young children get this point!

A bit of background to the writing of this story. Families tend to dislike notoriety of any kind, as it separates them from the rest of the community. This story was written by a member of a family that felt shame because one member was an alcoholic, at a time when alcoholism was not yet widely understood as an addiction. Alcoholism was thought to be sinful and wrong, the deliberate fault of the alcoholic who showed no concern or love for his/her family.

This story is not suggesting Jesus was an alcoholic. Rather, the writer has recognized a parallel between her feelings about an alcoholic family member, and the feelings that a younger sister may have had about her older brother as she perceives that people have strange reactions to him: "I don't really understand what is happening about Jesus." She pours out her growing resentment over some of Jesus' unconventional and unexpected actions (such as casting out demons, and his association with a prison inmate, John the Baptist) – actions which elicit teasing from her peers, despair from her parents, scorn and laughter from town folk, and shame for her family. Why can't Jesus be an ordinary brother? Rather than continue to be the object of everyone's pointed remarks, Jessica would rather disown Jesus as her brother. But she loves him too much, and it hurts too much to disown him.

Why'd he have to be my brother?

by Sybil Shaw Hamm, Steinbach, Manitoba

Jesus had a baby sister –
Was she always proud of him?
Doubt and shame afflicted her
Even though she was his kin.

"Fresh fish would be nice for your big brother's last supper," Momma says as she stirs the stew pot. My older brothers Abe, Daniel, and Jesus sit near the fire sharpening tools from Poppa's carpentry shop.

"Are you going fishing?" I ask the boys.

"Soon," they say.

"Can I go too?"

Abe groans, winks, says, "Isn't she too old to go with us? Shouldn't she be home preparing lentils for our soup?"

"I'm only eight," I remind him."Momma, please let me go. Jesus won't be here for me to go fishing with after today."

Jesus picks up a shawl off the floor, catches me in it, twirls me around the room. "What a lovely fish I've caught!"

"Stop it, "Momma says."Will there be fish here for supper or not?"

"Well, we'll be off then." And from the corner Daniel tosses me the basket for bringing home the catch.

Momma says,"Take the shawl, Jessica. It can get cool out on the lake."

Oh happy day! I'm going too!

My name is Jessica. Sometimes I wish I were not as old as eight. Sometimes I wish I were older. Sometimes I wish I had no brothers, but not today. Today I wish Jesus wouldn't go away. I think Momma and Poppa think that too, for Poppa won't speak right now to anyone, and Momma's talk sounds angry.

I don't really understand what is happening about Jesus. No

one tells me anything but I know something is wrong.

This morning I heard Momma say, "It's that gang of boys Jesus meets down by the boats. Since he started hanging around with them things haven't been the same."

Then Poppa said, "We should never have let him hike across the desert. He was there such a long time."

"Forty days," Momma said when Jesus did come home. Then before he even had his sandals off to wash his feet, she said, "Explain yourself, young man!"

I think Jesus should try harder not to worry Momma. I think Momma should leave Jesus alone sometimes. Of course, no one cares what I think.

In the morning Jesus leaves.

Goodbye, Jesus. Goodbye. See, now he's gone.

We all miss Jesus. When my aunt Elizabeth comes to visit she brings us news. She tells us, "People say Jesus is a preacher."

"I doubt it," says Poppa.

My brother Abe tells us that some people call Jesus a healer. Abe and Daniel have a good laugh at this.

"Which?" I ask Momma. "A preacher or a healer?"

Momma says all these stories are foolish.

"What then?"

She just sends me out to sweep the sawdust.

In the night I listen to Poppa comforting Momma, who is sobbing. Next day Poppa talks about cousin John, about him being in jail, about how Jesus will have to be more careful. Momma says she wishes Jesus would get a real job. Today my friend Philip Escarius tells me he heard that Jesus cured a person of a demon.

"Jesus is a demon," Sara Linus sings. She points her finger at me. "Sister of a demon. Sister of a demon..."

I say, "I'm going home."

I hate all this talk – Jesus, Jesus, Jesus. Some say "Jesus" and laugh. Others say, "Jesus is the new Messiah."

"What's a Messiah?" I ask, but nobody answers.

Today behind the synagogue, Daniel punches his best friend Paul Linus in the nose. Paul Linus says that Jesus is a madman.

Everyone is talking.

"Stop it," I want to scream at them all. Why do I have this Jesus for a brother anyway? I wish he'd vanish and everyone would forget him, and I could be Jessica, not "Jesus' little sister."

Here is the place I used to crawl into when Momma scolded me, where she keeps her spices. It's so cool. And dark. It smells like olive oil. I wonder if I can still fit in. Yes, I can.

I'll sit here awhile and think. I'd like to tell Jesus how all the talk makes me feel, how I feel like yelling, screaming as loud as I can. I'd like to tell him he's caused so much trouble that he's not my brother anymore.

I'd say, "Jesus..."

I'd say, "Jesus, you aren't..."

I'd say, "Jesus, you aren't my..."

I try to say it, here in the darkness, but it hurts too much.

The woman with a flow of blood

Mark 5:21–43

Restored to Community

For pre-teens and up

These two interdependent stories in Mark 5 deal with two women from very different backgrounds. Jairus' daughter comes from the very center of Jewish privilege ; the other, the woman with the flow of blood, from the extreme periphery of society, from the edge. Why does Mark intermingle the two stories?

Story #1 begins with Jairus, a big man at the synagogue, falling at Jesus' feet and begging help for his twelve-year-old daughter's life. He has followed Jesus to the seashore, along with a large crowd. Mark uses the Greek word *ochlos* to describe the crowd, indicating the oppressed and subjugated, unimportant street people who are on the edge, rather than *laos*.

Suddenly Story #1 is interrupted by Story #2. It is about a woman, a marginalized and nameless outcast who lives on the edge of society. It is almost as though Mark can't bear to complete Story #1 until Story #2 is told.

It is the interconnectedness of the two stories that I want to highlight.

Story #2 tells the story of a woman who is one of the *ochlos*. She has had a flow of blood for 12 years (!), has sought out many doctors, has spent all her money, is broke, desperate, and isolated from the community (as Leviticus 15:19–23 demands). She is a social reject and a victim of perpetual cultic impurity. No male kin is indicated. She is barren as well. Thus she is barred from participation in any aspect of the life of her city or synagogue. She is a victim of taboos. She is everywoman.

Traditionally, this passage has been treated in various ways:

1. It has not been addressed very often from the pulpit.
2. Dr. Lee Oo Chung, Korean theologian, says that when it is addressed from the pulpit, this passage is usually made to say that "humility, followed by obedience, is appropriate behavior for women." And therefore, by extension, for all people on the edge.
3. Usually the emphasis is on the woman's faith – "Your faith has made you whole." The extension, to all women, is that if you too had more faith, you too could be whole.
4. Often the emphasis is on Jesus the great healer. This ignores the fact that it was the woman who took the initiative in approaching him. She took her future into her own hands instead of knuckling under to social and religious expectations. It is true she sensed the liberating power of God in Jesus. But he did not approach her; rather, she took enormous personal risks to approach him.

I have always wondered why so many of the women who encountered Jesus seemed to be in need of healing. Wasn't there an able-bodied one among them? Why was this patriarchal bias so prominent in so many texts? My suspicions encouraged me to probe more deeply into the meaning of stories of Jesus' encounters with women.

This story, for example, may not entirely be about being "healed of a disease." Asian women claim the word translated "healed" is more properly translated as "liberated." The story may well be about the woman courageously breaking taboos ("this trouble") of tradition, culture, religion. She audaciously reaches out to Jesus in whom she senses liberation from her physical situation and spiritual isolation. By doing so, she violates religious law and transfers her own impurity to him.

Both the *New English Bible* and J.B. Phillips' translation render Mark 4:34 as "Go in peace (wholeness); free forever from this trouble." The "peace," the wholeness that Jesus speaks of, is not only spiritual, but socio-political. She is freed, liberated to participate in the life of the city, a place where a woman of the *ochlos* had no space at all. The "trouble" is not just the flow of blood, not simply a "disease," but the religious and social taboos to which this woman has been subjected, as well as the taboo against physical touching. It was by touch that the flow of blood was staunched. And in the end, too, in Story #1 it was by touch that the little girl was raised.

I think these two interconnected stories are both about being restored to community. Story #1 is about a young girl thought to be dead: "Your daughter is dead, why put the master to further trouble?" But she is restored to community by Jesus' touch. Story #2 is about a woman breaking the taboos of religion and culture, re-appropriating spiritual energy by touching Jesus, and being restored to community. When the setting free of the one at the edge is accomplished (Story #2), the setting free of the one at the center becomes possible (Story #1).

That interconnectedness needs to be emphasized. Those on the edge must be set free of their bondages before those at the center can live a life of wholeness. The relevant questions for us are:

1. Who are those on the edge in our society?
2. Are they being set free from their bondages?

Restored to community

A woman set free
From all her grief,
A girl raised up.
What a huge relief!

"My little girl is dying," the man cried out to Jesus. "She is only twelve years old. Will you come and touch her with your hands? Then she will get better and live." His voice rose above the sound of the waves on the lake.

Jesus followed Jairus, the president of the synagogue, to the center of town.

In the large crowd that jostled and shoved each other as they went about their business in the market was an unimportant woman who should not have been there at all. She'd had a flow of vaginal blood for twelve years. She was supposed to stay in her own house. People thought that anything or anyone she touched would be made "unclean." She had gone to many doctors. She had spent all her money. But she was getting no better. She couldn't have children. She was desperate.

She came up behind Jesus under cover of the crowd, thinking to herself, "If only I could touch him. If only I had the courage. I know it's forbidden for me to touch anyone, let alone a man. And I'm not even supposed to be out of my house. But if only I could touch this man, I think I could be set free to live my life in a new way."

She crept behind him. She stretched out her hand. But she only touched a woman standing beside Jesus. The crowd was so dense. She tried again. And then again. Finally, the tips of her fingers brushed his cloak. It was like a match being struck. It felt as if a fire exploded in her. She felt human again. She hadn't reached out to touch another human being deliberately for years. She felt her courage rise.

"Who touched me?" asked Jesus

"Jesus, don't be silly," answered one of his disciples. "There are so many people here bumping into each other. How can you possibly ask, 'Who touched me?'"

But Jesus turned back and searched through the crowd to see who had touched him. The woman was shaking like a leaf. She knew she had broken a taboo by touching another person. She was scared, but she felt a sudden flush of courage. So she took the risk. She flung herself down at Jesus' feet, and sobbed out her whole wretched story. How she had to stay in her own house for 12 years. How she had called in many doctors, and spent all her money. How she was no better, but worse. How she finally decided to try to touch him because she sensed his touch could raise her up to a new life.

Jesus reached out. He took the woman's hands. He raised her to her feet.

"Daughter," he said, "your willingness to take a risk has made you a different person. Go now as a whole person. You are free forever from this trouble."

Had she heard him properly? Free forever from this trouble? Free from living in loneliness? Free from jeers? Free from feeling dirty and unclean? Free from despair? Free from taboos?

While she stood there, astonished, messengers arrived from Jairus' house. "Your daughter is dead," they told Jairus. "There is no need to bother the master any further."

But Jesus said to them, "Just have some faith. Don't be afraid to risk."

Then he went with Peter, James, and John to Jairus' house. "Why are you making such a noise with your weeping and wailing?" he asked those crowding the bedroom. "The child is not dead. She is only asleep."

They hooted at this and jeered him.

Jesus cleared the crowd from the room. With only the girl's father and mother and his disciples with him, he went into the room where the child was.

Jesus reached out. He took the girl's hands. He raised her to her feet.

"Little girl, get up," he said. She stood up and walked around the room. The others nearly went out of their minds with joy.

All that Jesus said was, "She's hungry. Feed her."

Fifteen years later

Jairus' daughter in conversation with her friend Sarah

by Joan E. James
For children eight and up

Not yet a woman
Not still a child...
She found herself adrift until
A sense of worth her life did fill.

I don't know about you, Sarah, but I wouldn't want my childhood over again. Not my early teens anyway. I think it was the worst time of my life. I was so terrified of everything, mainly of growing up, really. But nobody would listen to my fears. There were so many things I wanted to ask my mother about, but she was always too busy, or didn't seem to want to answer my questions. I realize now she probably didn't know the answers herself.

My father was always kind but mostly away in the synagogue. In any case, they were not questions I could ask a man. My brother Joshua was two years older than me and everyone thought he was wonderful, especially my mother and my father. I loved him too and we played together a lot. He was very clever and could read the scriptures at a very early age. I wanted to read them too, but my father said it was not necessary for a girl to be able to read.

As he got older, Josh didn't want to play with me anymore. He spent a lot of time in the synagogue with my father. I had to help my mother do the cooking and serve my brother at table. We had servants but my mother always prepared the food. I became good at cooking; it was the one thing I did that received some notice and some praise.

But gradually I found that I didn't want to eat any of it. I pretended to eat it, of course. Nobody noticed for a long time that I had become very thin. I had no energy left and I knew in my heart of hearts that I really didn't want to go on living.

Eventually my family realized what was happening and tried to coax me to eat. But I couldn't, even to please my father. The thought of becoming a woman was unbearable to me; all that blood and uncleanness and being banished to the women's quarters every month. I couldn't face it, and I think my soul made the decision to depart from this life.

And then one day – I had been lying on my bed for over a month. I really felt as if I had died.

I was floating above my bed and saw myself lying there deathly white and still, and I saw everyone crying. My mother was in despair, rocking back and forth in her chair beside the bed.

But then I heard a voice call my name. It was if my body were calling me back very urgently and I had to obey it. Then I became aware of a rabbi sitting near me. He had a kind voice. He held my hand and talked to me for a long time about how lovely it was to be a grown woman and that I had nothing to fear from bleeding every month; that it was a sign of a healthy womb, capable of bearing children if I wanted them; that there was nothing unclean about womankind; that God loved me and everything about me. Sarah, he seemed to know, and answer, all those unanswered questions that had filled me with fear for so long.

And then he said something amazing. He said that I must love my body and everything about it, including my menstrual blood, because it is full of God. He said I am made of God-stuff, that we all are, and everything in the whole universe. And that's why we must look after ourselves and the world, because they are beautiful and sacred and full of God. And he said that's why I must decide to get better, so that I could sing and dance and enjoy life to the full.

He took my hand and said very kindly, "Young woman, sit up."

And do you know, Sarah, I knew at that moment that that was what I wanted to do. I sat up in bed and said, "I'm hungry."

The rabbi laughed and asked my mother to bring me something to eat. He looked so beautiful when he laughed that I just gazed and gazed at him. I knew at that moment I would love him all the days of my life. His name was Jesus of Nazareth.

You can imagine the effect of all this on my family. Their joy and their love for this man who had brought me back to them was overwhelming, and we begged him to make his home with us. But he said that he could not; that he had far to go, and not much time.

I never saw him again. But I'll remember him always.

Slightly adapted, by permission, from "Fifteen Years Later: Jairus' daughter in conversation with her friend Sarah," by Joan E. James, in *Celebrating Women*, edited by Hannah Ward, Jennifer Wild, and Janet Morley, 1995, SPCK.

Peter's denial

Mark 14:66–72; John 18:16–27

A woman's feeling

Two accounts are given of the same familiar incident, known usually as Peter's denial. In this story, our emphasis is on the woman slave who unmasked Peter and identified him as a follower of Jesus.

In most translations, the enslavement of women and men is glossed over. The Greek words *doule* and *doulos* are often translated as maidservant or manservant. Such a translation, according to theologian Luise Shottroff, conceals from the reader the true identity of the *kyrios*, the overlord of female and male slaves, who treated other human beings as subhumans, as things – as slaves. In the Greek Scriptures, the biblical stories often make the productive work of slaves invisible; they make it appear as though the work were done by the masters themselves. They hide from us the brutality of slavery.

The commentary of South African theologian Itumeleng Mossala makes the same point about the story of Esther in the Hebrew Scriptures. The biblical story neither condemns the use of forced labor (Esther 10:1–3), nor does it mention the slave labor that built the lavish court of the king of Persia (Esther 1). The whole issue of class struggle is suppressed, thereby raising the question of the class character and the ideological bias of this text.

The high priest's female slave, on whom this story is based, worked in the courtyard of the palace. She did not just "happen to be there." One of her duties was to keep the fire going, and to open the gate to those seeking admittance. She would want to keep a sharp eye out for intruders, to curry favor with her owner, the high priest. To him, she owed her primary allegiance. She had few choices.

It's easy for us, too, to overlook and

underestimate slaves. This one was a perceptive person. Not only was she fully aware of the Jesus movement ("You too were with Jesus, the man from Nazareth.") but she also suspected that Peter was "one of them." We can imagine her whispering with the others in the courtyard about how his Galilean accent betrayed his identity. Finally, she decides to go with her feelings, and she unmasks him.

For further reading

Mosala, Itumeleng J. *Biblical Hermeneutics & Black Theology in South Africa.* Wm. B. Eerdmans, Grand Rapids, MI, 1989.

Shottroff, Luise. *Lydia's Impatient Sisters: a Feminist Social History of Early Christianity.* Westminster/John Knox Press, Louisville, KY, 1995.

A woman's feeling

One of them, fee fee fye.
One of them, you can't deny!

I had a feeling he was "one of them." He came through the palace gate, with his friend. The friend knows my master, the high priest. Since I was on duty at the gate, I had to check on everyone who came into the courtyard. I asked him, "Are you one of that man's disciples?"

I meant Jesus, of course. He was the reason that all the high priests were meeting through the night. He was causing such a disturbance for us. Ordinarily, the gates would be locked up at night, and I could sleep, to get ready for tomorrow's duties. But tonight, I had to work through the night. And I knew I should warn my master if any of this troublemaker's disciples tried to get into the yard. It was my duty to my master.

The big man replied, "No! I don't know who you're talking about."

I didn't believe him. I just had a feeling. He was trying to save his own skin. I had a strong feeling he was the same man I'd heard about last night.

My friend Malchus, one of the male slaves of the high priest, and his fellow guards had been ordered to arrest this Jesus. They'd traced him to the darkness of an olive orchard, outside the walls of the city. There'd been a fight. One of Jesus' right-hand men had a sword with him. When he saw the palace guards taking Jesus by force, he lost his temper. He took out his sword and laid into the guards. Malchus struck back, of course. It got pretty wild. I heard the Malchus had his ear cut right off. He had run out of the garden, screaming and yelling for help.

I heard gossip in the palace that they might turn Jesus over to Pilate, the Roman governor. They're afraid of him. Jesus has so many followers, the guards here couldn't stop them if they rioted.

That's why I asked this big man coming through the gate if he was "one of them." The children in the courtyard heard me. They started to chant:

"One of them, fee fee fye,
One of them, you can't deny!"

A little later, I was stoking up the fire. I noticed the big man come close to warm himself. He stretched out his palms to the flames. I whispered to some of the others hanging around the fire, "I have a feeling this fellow is one of them." Everyone knew what I meant. Jesus and his followers were the talk of the whole town.

Then one of the crowd said it out loud, pointing at him. The children took up the chant again:

"One of them, fee fee fye,
One of them, you can't deny!"

He said again, "No! You're mistaken!"

The cousin of Malchus whispered to me that he was certain this was the man who had cut off Malchus' ear the night before. Another friend in the crowd whispered to me: "His accent betrays him. He's from Galilee. He speaks the way all those from Galilee speak."

I stared at the big man. But he wouldn't look me in the eye. I had a strong feeling he was "one of them." He kept hanging around, waiting for news of the trial going on inside.

The children kept up their chant:

"One of them, fee fee fye,
One of them, you can't deny!"

More and more, I had a feeling he was the man I thought he was. So I decided to challenge him again. "You **are** one of them for sure. You are a Galilean. I can tell by your accent."

He began to curse and swear. He was so mad at being found out. "I do not know the man you speak of," he bellowed at me. He meant Jesus, of course. But it was a silly lie. Everyone in the city knew of Jesus by now.

I was so upset at his yelling at me. And to tell the truth, I was a bit scared, too. I was ready to burst into tears. Then two things happened.

A cock crew. It must have been near dawn already. And the big man, who scared me with his bigness and bluster, suddenly stared around and then burst into tears. He held his head in his hands, as if he was totally ashamed of himself. He cried very hard. I don't think he heard the children. They kept up their chant, pointing fingers at him:

"One of them, fee fee fye,
One of them, you can't deny!"

I had a strong feeling all along he was one of them. Now it was clear that he was. I had nothing against this big man. I'm only a slave. But it was my duty to report to my master anyone suspicious who came into the courtyard. And I had a feeling all along the big man was one of them.

The bakerwoman

Matthew 13:33; Luke 13:20 ff.

By a woman's hands

The brief parable of the leaven appears in both Matthew's and Luke's gospels. Its significance is that God's reign is to be compared to leaven that a woman took and hid in three measures of flour, until all the meal was leavened. God is not the woman baking bread, nor is the bread holy. But God's actions in the world become visible in this work that a woman does to keep life going. God works in the world to make life possible for us in very ordinary ways, in the same way that the woman baking bread works to sustain life.

The poverty of the people in 1st century Palestine is the context for the parable. For women, even today, in the Two-Thirds World, the product of mixing flour with yeast is the raw material of life itself. Bread is the symbol for being able to live.

One of my earliest childhood memories of the Depression years of the 1930s was searching the extensive church lawn in case someone had dropped five cents. A nickel. At that time, a nickel would by a loaf of bread. If I had found five cents, I planned on buying a loaf and eating all of it myself!

The parable of the leaven makes ordinary women's work a picture of God's reign. It confers great significance on this woman's work. It makes her work visible, placing it on the same level as men's work. Bread and God, the hands of a woman baking bread and the hands of God, are brought into relation.

Many interpreters of this parable have never made bread. Many have never even looked inside a cookbook! Their interpretations tend to overlook that it was a woman who "took" and "hid" the yeast. If the parable were only about the rising process (which is the traditional interpretation), it would have been sufficient to talk about yeast and a kneading machine. In Roman Palestine, bread was baked in bakeries. But here the emphasis is on the hard work of the woman kneading the dough, as well as on the waiting for the dough to rise.

The action and the waiting belong together, as God reveals God's self in the midst of ordinary life.

For further reading

Shottroff, Luise. *Lydia's Impatient Sisters, a Feminist Social History of Early Christianity.* Westminster/John Knox Press, Louisville, KY, 1995.

By a woman's hands

Work and wait, work and wait
The dough will soon fulfill its fate.
A loaf of bread for one and all,
God's reign is like that, you recall.

My mom was making bread. I knew it the minute I came home. I could smell it. Mom was the best baker in our shantytown. We had a huge mud-brick oven, so she baked bread for five families, every second day. We only had one meal a day. Bread was the main thing we ate. That, with rice and beans when we could get them.

I knew she had taken the yeast and dissolved it in lukewarm water. I imagined how she had poured this over some of the flour, hiding it, and stirred it into a thick paste. I remembered helping her, by throwing three handfuls of flour over the mixture. Then we set it in bowls, and covered it, and let it rise until the next morning.

That's what I smelled right away when I came home. It tickled my nose. My stomach rumbled. I knew we would have fresh bread to eat tomorrow.

Now all we had to do was wait. It's hard to wait. We weren't the only ones waiting. I guess everyone in our shantytown was waiting too.

"We smell bread, bread, wonderful bread;
Sometime tomorrow we'll all be fed,"

chanted the kids from all the houses nearby. We played in a circle, pretending to knead the dough in an imaginary bowl. It was a game we often played while waiting for our bread.

But in the morning, the really hard work began. All the remaining flour had to be kneaded into the leavened batter with our hands. That's hard work. Mom let me do some of it. My little fists get tired, kneading the dough. But Mom never tired. I was always amazed watching her hands: up and down, in and out, up and down, in and out... Such hard work!

"We smell bread, bread, wonderful bread;
Sometime tomorrow we'll all be fed,"
chanted the kids.

The dough was covered. We waited calmly. We all knew we had a long time to wait. The yeasty part of the dough had to have time to work on the rest of the flour. We had to trust the yeast to do its work. Nothing we could do ourselves would raise the dough into a sweet smelling loaf. My mom had done her work.

"We smell bread, bread, wonderful bread;
Sometime tomorrow we'll all be fed,"
chanted the kids.

After a few hours my mom slid the bread into the huge oven. Then the delicious smell became overpowering. It tickled our noses. Our stomachs rumbled. We knew we would have bread today.

"We smell bread, bread, wonderful bread;
Sometime ***today*** *we'll all be fed,"*
chanted the kids.

Violence against women

The Levite's concubine

Judges 19:1–30, 20:1–17 and 35–37

Long hair and round deep eyes

For teens

A Levite goes to retrieve his concubine from her father's house, and then allows her to be raped and left for dead. Then he dismembers her. He seems to have no sense of who she was as a person, nor of her loyalties or her life or her wishes. It is a story of unrelenting horror. Read it in Judges 19–20.

What possible redeeming value has this story? On the surface, none. The story is like a tribunal. It has been written for posterity, for all to consider, to take counsel, to speak out.

The concubine had no voice to protest, but we are called by this text to be her voice against the violence inflicted on women and children. To listen and learn from it may help to ensure that it does not continue to be repeated over and over again in our time. Bear in mind that in our time, violence against women (verbal, physical, spiritual, economic, political) is the thread that binds women commonly around the world. It is rampant. Women have survived war and rape in Bosnia and Palestine; forced feeding in Mauritania; sexual trafficking in Romania and China. Women are still being captured, betrayed, raped, tortured, murdered, dismembered, and scattered even in Canada.

The story is set in the period of the Judges, when chaos abounded. It was told to undercut Saul's kingship and to support a strong central rule under David. But simply to advocate a political solution does not address the horror of this story. Not only is the life of a powerless innocent woman taken violently, but it becomes the prelude and excuse for the massacre of the people of Benjamin and the violation of the virgin women of Shiloh and Jabesh-Gilead. The slaughter of one defenseless woman escalates into the slaughter and violation of hundreds of defenseless persons. Violence begets violence.

In the story the men speak to each other. The women are silent. They are the property of men.

If you have access to Carol Lynn Pearson's video, *Mother Wove the Morning*, review it.

Vestiges of the attitudes in such stories often still shape contemporary situations. "Who gives this woman...?" was used until very recently in marriage ceremonies, as women were passed from father to husband. In abusive home situations, the scripture "Submit yourself to your husband," is still too often quoted to the woman. Reformation leader John

Calvin advised battered women to try harder and to pray more. Christian vocabulary abounds in metaphors of the Church as a wife (imperfect) and God as husband/lover (perfect). One familiar hymn has, "From heaven he came and sought her, to be his holy bride; with his own blood he bought her..."

The lack of mutuality is bad news for women.

Many women believe that suffering is God's will, and that violence against them is their fault. Sexual and violent abuse is rampant. Many very young children know all about it.

Should this story of outrageous horror be told to children? Yes. To refrain from telling it would be to acquiesce in the historic cover-up of this violence. It must be stopped.

For further reading

Gnanadason, Aruna. *No Longer Silent: Violence Against Women Worldwide.* World Council of Churches, Geneva, 1993

Pearson, Carol Lynn. *Mother Wove the Morning.* Video or book, available through 1384 Cornwall Crt., Walnut Creek, CA 94596, or through AVEL.

Trible, Phyllis. *Texts of Terror.* Fortress, Philadelphia, 1984.

Long hair and round deep eyes

They raped her, they beat her
They cut her in bits.
This kind of behavior
Should give us all fits.

You don't really want to hear this story. But I must tell it.

It happened when I was only 13 years old, a long time ago. I am an old woman now, but I can remember every detail as though it were yesterday. It was in the days when there was no king in our country and terrible things happened to people.

I lived in Gibeah, which belongs to the tribe of Benjamin. One day my father brought home with him a Levite priest. He was dressed grandly with rich robes. My father said to my mother, "This Levite priest is a stranger in our town. He has no place to stay, so I have asked him to be my guest – he and his donkeys and his woman."

My father and the priest got drinking and telling jokes.

The young woman with the priest stayed in the kitchen with my mother and me. She was just four years older than I was – and much younger than the withered old Levite priest. She told us she lived in Bethlehem of Judah. She had long hair and round deep eyes, smooth smooth skin and a sad face. She never smiled.

Her father, she said, had sold her to the Levite priest. Sold her, like a piece of furniture. But she hated the priest and ran away from him, back to Bethlehem, to her father's house. The Levite came after her. When she saw him arrive at her home, she cried and wept. Her father wouldn't protect her – after all, he had already sold her. So she was loaded onto the Levite's donkey, and tied on so she couldn't run away again. They had traveled a long time. She couldn't do anything else but stay with him now. Where was there to run if her own father turned her out?

I put my arm around her. I quietly sobbed with her and stroked her long hair. She thanked me with her round deep eyes.

That night, about midnight, there were loud knocks on the door. I heard some men yelling, "Bring us the stranger who is staying here tonight." They were from the tribe of Benjamin.

"No," answered my father. "I cannot. He is my guest."

"Bring him," they yelled louder.

Suddenly the door of my bedroom flew open. My father grabbed me with one hand and the Levite's young woman with the other. He half dragged us to the door of our house. "Look," he shouted at the men, "Here is my daughter, a young girl, and a young woman with long hair and round deep eyes. She belongs to the man you want to abuse. Do whatever you like with these two young girls, but the man who is my guest is a priest – a man of God. Spare him."

His shouting wakened my mother. She came racing after us, her nightdress billowing. She gathered us both in her arms and cried defiantly at my father, "Leave these girls alone!"

The three of us ran out the back door. Though my legs were shaking and trembling with fright, we ran to a hill behind our house and hid. It was only when I was safely hidden among the rocks that I realized the Levite's young woman had tripped and been caught. My mother and I heard her screaming. We watched with horror as she was carried by the men to the edge of the hill where we hid. They didn't know we were there, and we had to put our hands over our mouths to keep from screaming ourselves.

Then it happened. It was terrible. They laid her on the ground. Two of them held her hands and arms. Two held her feet. She couldn't move. Then they abused her. They laughed and tried to outdo each other with their mean and disgusting behavior. My mother held me close and whispered to me to look up at the moon, not at what was happening before our eyes.

Finally the dawn came. The men left. The young woman crawled to the door of our house. When she reached the door, she collapsed. Her long hair spilled over the door frame. She couldn't go any further.

The Levite came out of the door and saw her. "Up," he said,

prodding her with his foot. "We must be going."

She didn't answer. He spoke again. She still did not answer. He bent down and poked her. He rose up again, and said, "She's dead. Bring the donkey."

I couldn't believe it. She might as well have been a stick of wood for all he cared about her as a person.

But he cared about her as his property. I learned later that when this Levite got to his own home, he took the body of his young women and carved her up into 12 parts. He sent one piece to each tribe of Israel, with a message calling for vengeance against the tribe of Benjamin. He and the warriors of his own tribe went on a rampage. They killed hundreds of defenseless women in their thirst for revenge, for the way in which the men of Benjamin had treated the Levite's "property" – that young woman who died in front of our house. The wives of all the men of the whole tribe of Benjamin were murdered too.

They didn't do it to honor the memory of the young woman with the long hair and round deep eyes. Oh no. They did it because the Levite felt insulted by a few men of Benjamin for destroying his "property."

For years after, whenever I heard my father boast of how he saved the life of a man of God, I put my hands over my ears and left the room. I cried. I remembered the young woman with the long hair and the round deep eyes. My father never mentioned the huge numbers of women who were senselessly killed as a result of that one night's violence. And for what?

Now that I'm an old woman and can say exactly what I want, I wonder sometimes if there is a God? And if there is, why didn't She act?

Michal, the king's daughter

2 Samuel 3:13–17; 2 Samuel 6:12–23

It wasn't fair

For pre-teens and up

A good Israelite wife never attempted to rule her husband, nor oppose him publicly. An ideal wife deferred to him in speech and action, obeyed his wishes, and put his welfare first. This story is about Michal, a wife who had consistently put David's welfare first, but who finally rebelled against the abuse her husband David heaped on her, despite the cost to herself. Though she was the daughter of King Saul and wife of King David, she was used as a possession and treated as a political pawn.

She is a minor character in the story of the two mighty kings, but she nevertheless played a significant role in their story. Saul's kingship had been rejected by God, the Bible story tells us, and David was waiting in the wings. Saul, hopelessly jealous of David, tried to use his daughter Michal as bait to lure David to his death. But through Michal's intervention, David escaped from Saul. (For background here, read "Michal," page 125 in *Miriam, Mary and Me.*) When David did not return to Michal, Saul gave her in marriage to another man, Paltiel, who loved her dearly.

David never gave up his desire to be king. He knew that if he could get Michal back again, then the people would acclaim him as king (2 Samuel 3:14–17). She, a king's daughter, would legitimize his claim to Saul's throne. Royal women imparted power to the men who would be king. To claim a king's harem was to claim his throne. So he took her forcibly from Paltiel. This political agenda lay behind what appears to be only a domestic dispute in 2 Samuel 6:12–23.

Michal never forgave David for using her to climb up the ladder of power. He had never returned to claim her, after she had saved his life. He was in fact made king at last (2 Samuel 5:4). This is the background for our story.

Michal was so outraged by the way David had mistreated her to grab the throne that she finally exploded emotionally, and in public too. When she saw him entering Jerusalem "wearing [nothing but] a linen ephod, dancing without restraint before the Lord... she despised him in her heart "(2 Samuel 6:14–16). She scornfully addressed him as "the king of Israel." Her challenge was not so much about his being scantily clad before the women, but about occupying a throne that should have remained in her family.

The record has her standing alone, isolated from the other women. She challenged him and she lost. Her relationship with David came to a bitter end. David had the last word, because he had the power. Her final "punishment" was the bleak line, "Michal, Saul's daughter, had no child to her dying day." Symbolically, depriving her of children was the equivalent of murder. She was written out of the record. Forever.

For further reading

Exum, Cheryl J. "Murder They Wrote" in *Union Seminary Quarterly Review*, 50th Anniversary volume, New York, p. 19.

Hackett, Jo Anne. "Samuel 1 and 2," *Women's Bible Commentary*, ed. Carol A. Newsom and Sharon H. Ringe. Westminster/John Knox Press, Louisville, KY, 1992.

Laffey, Alice. *An Introduction to the Old Testament: a Feminist Perspective.* Fortress Press, Philadelphia, 1988, p. 108.

It wasn't fair

Michal was courageous,
Michal was brave,
Though she failed in her effort
Not to be David's slave.

Michal thought she would never see her husband David again. In fact, she didn't see him for years and years. So her father King Saul gave her away to another man called Paltiel, who loved her very much. Paltiel always gave her figs instead of dates for breakfast, because he knew she loved figs.

David had always wanted to be king. After a few years, he did become king. But only king of some of the people, not of all of Israel. He knew that if he could get Michal back again from Paltiel, her new husband, then all the rest of the people would accept him as their king too. She was, after all, the daughter of King Saul!

It didn't seem to matter to him that he didn't love her.

One day he rode to Paltiel's camp. He took along 40 of his strongest fighters. "Hand over to me my wife Michal, Saul's daughter," he thundered. One of his big bullies wrenched her away from her husband and threw her over his shoulder like a sack of flour.

Paltiel loved her very much, but he couldn't stop David. He and his men weren't strong enough. Paltiel trailed along. He followed David's men and Michal, their prisoner, as far as he could, crying and shouting all the way. "Give her back. She's mine!" bawled Paltiel.

David ignored him.

It wasn't fair! Michal shouted, cried, and shrieked her protests at David's men. There was nothing she could do either.

Finally David's men made Paltiel go home without Michal. It wasn't fair at all.

They took Michal to David's house. Michal moaned. She cried. She grumbled. She sulked. She bellowed at David. She was so mad, she roared at him. She picked up a hand mirror off her table and hurled it to the floor where it splintered into a thousand fragments. She no longer loved him. He had never come back to her, even though she had once saved his life. Now he had wrenched her from Paltiel like a bag of flour. She hated him now. She was his wife again, even though she didn't want to be.

It wasn't fair at all.

Just the same, David finally did become King David. After he defeated his enemies, 30,000 of his soldiers came with him in a celebration parade to Jerusalem, called the City of David. They brought with them The Ark of God, a beautifully carved box that held the precious laws of the Israelites. It was mounted on a cart. They wheeled it along the parade route through the city, where the people stood at the side of the road and cheered.

David and all the people danced and sang with joy for the victory they believed God had given them.

The cymbals clashed;

The tambourines jingled and jangled;

The castanets clacked the rythym.

The music of the lutes floated above the crowd's noise.

Michal was watching the parade through a window of her home. She saw David, his clothing stripped down to his waist, leaping and dancing half-naked before all the people. She clenched her fists and hung her head in despair. She detested David. She had suffered so badly at his hands. She started to cry. He had used her to get what he wanted – to be King of Israel.

It just wasn't fair.

Why should she sit back and let David misuse her? She turned her anger to boldness. She screwed up her courage and decided to do something.

When David came back to the palace, Michal went out to meet him in the street. Instead of cheering him as the other women were doing, she jeered him in her loud commanding voice. Everyone could hear: "What a fine reputation the King of Israel has won himself today, acting like an empty-headed fool in front of all the slave girls."

It was the first time she ever had called him "the King of Israel." The crowd knew she was mocking him. And David knew she was taunting him.

David yelled back angrily, "I was made king in the presence of God, who chose me over your father and over his family. God appointed me Prince over Israel and over the people of God. If I want to dance in the streets, I will do it, and other women will honor me for it."

The crowd turned against her. Michal ran back into her house. She was silenced. She was bitter.

She wished she were dead. She might as well have been. Nobody listened to her. Nobody cared. She spent the rest of her life sitting alone in the corner of her room in David's harem. David never visited her. She had no children. No one talked to her.

But David became the unchallenged ruler of all of Israel.

It wasn't fair at all.

Susanna

Daniel Chapter 13 (New Jerusalem Bible) and in the Apocryphal Additions to the *Book of Daniel (New Revised Standard Version)*

Falsely accused

For children age nine and up

This is a subversive piece of literature, satirizing the Jewish "establishment," according to André LaCocque. In this case, the elders or scribes claim that those who do not live in accordance with the prescriptions of the Torah are unworthy to have a part in the community. So far, the rabbis are in full agreement. But these very elders, on whose authority the community relies, turn out to be adulterous (verse 14), bring false accusation (verse 62), disregard the innocent (verse 60), and are wicked (verse 62). It is a story of betrayal, treachery, violation of trust, and misused power. In the end, truth prevails. The wicked elders lose their lives, and the righteous are acquitted.

The story (probably historical fiction, like the books of Ruth and Esther) comes out of the underground literature of the 1st–2nd century BCE. The stories of Susanna and Judith are often not included in Protestant Bibles, though they are part of the Hebrew Scriptures. Read the chapter in the Bible before you try to tell this story.

Susanna is a well-to-do Jew, virtuous and beautiful. Her name (which means "lily") is used to evoke the beautiful woman of the Song of Songs. She is married to a wealthy and esteemed man, Joakim. Two elders see her walking about her garden and lust after her. They then plot to satisfy their lust, confronting her with the choice of having sexual intercourse with them or, if she refuses, of public accusation of the same (Daniel 13:15–21). The law required only two witnesses for a judgment that could lead to capital punishment. (Deuteronomy 17:6). Susanna refuses. She is accused, and is being taking to her death when young Daniel intervenes. Cross-examining the scribes, Daniel asks them near which tree in the garden the alleged adultery took place. When they give different answers, their lie is exposed (Daniel 13:47–59). They are then executed, since transgressors of the laws of the Torah merit death.

Through this story, the storyteller underlines the hypocrisy of the religious establishment. The story teaches that religious authority lies not in skillful exegesis of the Torah by the elders, but in Susanna's faithfulness to the laws of the Torah and in trusting God's spirit to hear her cries.

The storyteller also singles out the young child Daniel as the one who teaches the elderly guardians of tradition. Wisdom often lies with the insights of the young, not the sages. Daniel seems a child, but to God he is a prophet. His wisdom is a gift of the Spirit. This was a direct criticism of those elders/scribes of Judaism, who claimed that prophecy ceased with Haggai and Malachi. Daniel is able to recognize injustice before any proof of guilt is produced, moved as he is by prophetic inspiration.

The story is about sexual intimidation and false accusation of the innocent by those in power positions: elders who have been appointed by the people as judges. Remember, it's a story, not a factual account of the Hebrew judicial system! Susanna represents the innocent victim of systemic injustice in religion and society, on trial to prove herself innocent. It may remind you of rape cases in Canada. Or, as in the wretched stories of Canadian Indian residential schools of a past era, of a few religious authorities who betrayed their trust and have finally been accused in their turn by the victims.

Note that in the biblical account, Daniel does not come to the rescue of the woman, but of the "righteous." It is a story in which truth and justice prevail. Wisdom and righteousness triumph (note the pairing of Daniel and Susanna). Hypocritical wrongdoers are punished, and virtuous folk are vindicated.

For further reading

Bellis, Alice Ogden. *Helpmates, Harlots, Heroes: Women's Stories in the Hebrew Bible.* Westminster/John Knox, Louisville, KY, 1994.

LaCocque, André, *The Feminine Unconventional,* Fortress Press, MN, 1990, pp. 27 ff.

Falsely accused

Susanna, Susanna, good and pure,
The man who charged you was a boor,
Susanna, Susanna, we know you're true,
Today, we expect, you'd want to sue!

It's not easy being beautiful. I sometimes wonder if the stories of my beauty that people pass around caused my trial? Or was it because I married Joakim who is very rich and respected, and others were jealous?

Here's what happened.

Two of the elders of my people were appointed judges. They came to our house every morning to hold court and decide cases. They were supposed to guide the people. The people trusted them.

Every noon hour, after the people had left, I walked in my husband's garden. I loved the scents of the flowers and the songs of the birds. One fine day I went into the garden as usual with no one but my two maids. I decided to bathe in the garden because it was so hot.

"Bring me olive oil and soap and towels, and close the doors of the garden so that I can bathe alone," I told my maids.

They did as I bid them. After they had brought the things I had requested, they went out and shut the doors of the garden. I began to take off my clothes..

Suddenly, the two male elders appeared. I grabbed a towel to cover myself. I trembled with fear. I broke out in a sweat. My tongue stuck to the top of my dry mouth.

"The doors of your garden are shut and no one can see us," they told me. "We want to have sex with you. If you say no, we will swear that there was a young man with you here in the garden, and that was why you dismissed your maids."

I thought to myself, "I am in a very tight place. I will not do as they ask. But if I refuse them, and they lie about me, it means my death, according to the laws of my religion. But I would rather say no than do what is wrong in God's sight."

I screamed as loudly as I could. The two men shouted even louder. One of them ran and flung open the garden gates. When the people in the house heard the shouting in the garden they all rushed through the side door to see what had happened to me.

The elders told their side of the story. My maids didn't know what to think, because nothing like this had ever been said against me. I couldn't speak, because I was shaking so, but also because I knew it was my word against theirs. They were respected elders.

I couldn't sleep all night long even though Joakim tried to comfort me. I went over and over what had happened. I knew I was not guilty. But I was terrified. I had nightmares. The two elders appeared in my nightmare as two huge animals who wanted to eat me. I woke up screaming.

The next day the people gathered for my trial. And the same two wicked elders were the judges who would decide my case. They shouted, "Send for Susanna, the wife of Joakim."

The officials came and got me. I had to come. I came with my parents, my children, and all my relatives. Joakim was present of course, but helpless. I was so ashamed, even though I knew I was not guilty. People had told me I was very beautiful, so I modestly wore a veil so that every passer-by would not stare at me. Now they ordered me to lift my veil, something that was never done with women like me. I felt like dirt. All the women who were there started to cry in sympathy for me. I broke down and sobbed.

There was so much pain in my heart. All I could do was silently beg God to save me from more disgrace.

I felt the hands of the two elders on my head, and they spoke.

"As we were walking by ourselves in the garden," they said, "this woman came in with two maids, shut the door of the garden, and dismissed her maids. A young man who had been hidden came to her and lay down with her. And we were in the corner of the garden and when we saw this wicked action we ran up to them, and though we saw them together, we could not hold him because he was younger and stronger than we were. He opened the gates and rushed out. We immediately laid hold of this woman and asked her who the young man was. She would not tell us. This is our true word. We swear it is the truth."

I heard gasps and sighs and mutterings. I knew that many of the people believed the two men because they were elders of the people, appointed as judges. They were supposed to guide the people. They condemned me to death, which was the law.

I screamed, "God, you know what they have accused me of is false. Here I am to die when I have done none of the things they have charged me with." The people had to support me by holding my arms because I was too faint to stand. They were leading me away to be put to death. What injustice! I screamed again and again, but no one did anything to save me. They couldn't. They believed the elders.

But then God heard my cries, and stirred up the holy spirit of a young man. I heard a voice cry out, "I am clear about the innocence of this woman."

The people turned to the young man. His name was Daniel. The people demanded, "What do you mean?"

"Are you such fools that you would condemn a woman without really examining the story that has been told about her?" he asked. "These men have lied about her. Let us return to the court and review the case," the young man urged.

So they did. The two elders invited the young man to speak.

"Separate the two elders from each other, and I will ask them questions," said Daniel.

To the first one he asked, "Under which tree did you see her meet the young man in her garden?"

The elder answered, "Under a mastic tree."

He ordered the other judge be brought to him. "Under which tree did you catch them hugging and kissing?" he asked.

"Under a live oak tree," answered the judge.

"You have both lied," shouted Daniel. "Your own mouths have proved you are liars." And he turned them over to the crowd to do with them as they wished. And the crowd put them to death for lying.

My husband Joakim was in tears. He was so glad I had been proved righteous. My mother and father and all who loved me hugged and kissed me. We celebrated with a huge feast that night. Daniel was the guest of honor. And I said a prayer of thanksgiving to God such has never been heard in the land before!

Tricksters

Rebekah

Genesis 24–27

Pulling the wool over Isaac's eyes

A story for children eight and up

Who is Rebekah? She is a puzzle for modern-day readers. Why did she favor one son over another? Was she a strong and virtuous woman who responded to God's call? Or was she a demonic deceiver ? Was her trickery/deception justified? Did she fight fairly against patriarchal institutions? Were her choices honorable, given the constraints of her culture?

The wife of Isaac, she bears the twins Jacob and Esau. In a dream, God reveals to her that the older will serve the younger (Genesis 25:22–23). Isaac prefers Esau the hunter; Rebekah believes that God prefers Jacob the homebody.

The relevant episode for us is Rebekah's deception of Isaac over his blessing. He intends to give the blessing to Esau, but Rebekah persuades Jacob to deceive the old man. Jacob convinces Isaac that he is really Esau, the older son. Rebekah herself will take the consequences, she says (Genesis 27:5–13). Esau's subsequent anger compels Rebekah to hustle Jacob out of the way to her brother Laban for safety.

Most traditional interpretations depict Rebekah's most serious sin as deceiving her husband Isaac. But did not Isaac also deceive and trick without being chastised (Genesis 26:1–7)? The offense here to traditional interpreters is that the woman is the trickster.

She succeeds in her plans through sex's symbolic counterpart – food. She does not trick to retaliate against Isaac's previous deception. She tricks because it is the only option open to her in a patriarchal society. She wins by moving the men around like chess pieces. Hers is the vicarious power of mockery, humor, and deception – although not that of a liberated woman. After all, what is at stake is her son's status, not her own. Given the nature of her society and the powerlessness women experienced in it, trickery was her only option.

Feminists point out that Rebekah's dream revealed to her that Jacob would be the one to shape the future of her people. So she must participate by courageously acting, not merely by giving birth. Abraham had been asked to sacrifice Isaac. Could not Rebekah be asked to sacrifice her marriage trust?

Some see her reason for favoring Jacob as her attempt to live out God's intentions. Others see it as her effort to uphold Mesopotamian customs, in which the younger child inherited.

In any case, she remains the subordinate woman who must do the best she can within male structures. People in secondary positions often resort to what the dominant group considers deception in order to survive. This does not justify, but it may explain, the trickery. She was definitely in the tradition of Israelite tricksters. They tended to imagine themselves as underdogs who achieved success in subversive ways. Their trickery (or deception) always involved transformation or change. It was usually carried out by younger sons who would inherit, by women, or by Israelites in foreign lands – all of whom had to overcome great odds. Within the confines of a male patriarchy, Rebekah may have been just such a one.

For further reading

Newsom and Ringe. *The Women's Bible Commentary.* Westminster/John Knox, Louisville, KY, 1992, p. 19 ff.

Bellis, Alice Ogden. *Helpmates, Harlots, Heroes: Women's Stories in the Hebrew Bible.* Westminster/John Knox, Louisville, KY, 1994.

Pulling the wool over Isaac's eyes

So little that I can do
But what I can I will,
A blessing for my younger son
Should nicely fit the bill.

I overheard my husband calling Esau. "Go catch some game for me. Then fix it in a tangy dish. I want to bless you before I die," said old Isaac.

Immediately I called Esau's twin brother Jacob.

"Listen to me, my son, and do what I tell you," I said. "Quickly, bring me some venison and I will make a tangy dish for your father, the kind he likes. Then you take it in to your father. He is old and blind and will not be able to tell who it is. He'll think you are your brother Esau. He will eat the food and bless you before he dies."

I couldn't think of any other way to get around Isaac. He had firmly fixed in his mind that the oldest boy should receive the inheritance, even if that wasn't God's plan. I knew the plan, because in a dream God showed me that Esau the elder will serve Jacob the younger. The only way for our clan to survive is to make sure that Jacob gets Isaac's blessing. There is no other way. So I'll do whatever it takes.

Isaac won't like it, but we women have so little say in what goes on among the men. I have no choice but to support Jacob by going behind Isaac's back. He wouldn't listen to me if I came right out and said what I think.

"Come on, mother," objected Jacob." My brother Esau is a hairy man. My skin is smooth. If my father feels me, he will know I am tricking him and he will curse me instead of blessing me."

"Leave it to me, son," I reassured him. "I'll take the consequences from your father."

"Come on, mother," objected Jacob again." My brother Esau is an outdoors man. He smells of woodsmoke all the time. If my father smells me, he will know I am tricking him and he will curse me instead of blessing me."

"Leave it to me, son," I reassured him. "I'll take the consequences from your father."

It's up to me to pass the inheritance of our clan to Jacob, not up to Isaac. I am the one who knows what God wants.

Jacob did as I told him. He is more his mother's son than his father's. I fixed a meal, dressed Jacob in Esau's best clothes, put goatskins on his hands and the smooth nape of his neck, and sent him with the tangy dish to his father Isaac.

"Father," he called.

"Yes, my son. Who are you?" his blind father answered.

"I am Esau, your eldest son," answered Jacob. "I have done as you told me. Sit up and eat some of my venison. Then you may give me your blessing."

But the old man was suspicious. Isaac said to Jacob, "Why are you back so soon?"

"It is what God put in my way," Jacob responded.

"Come closer and let me feel you, my son, to see whether you really are my son Esau." When Jacob came close, Isaac felt him. "The voice is Jacob's voice, but his hands are Esau's. Are you really my son Esau?" he demanded suspiciously.

"Yes I am," answered Jacob.

"Then bring me some of your tangy dish that I may give you my blessing," said Isaac.

Jacob brought it to him and he ate it. Jacob brought wine too, and he drank it.

Then his father Isaac said, "Come near, my son, and kiss me." When Jacob came near and kissed him, Isaac smelt the woodsy smell of Esau's clothes. Then Isaac blessed my son Jacob:

"The smell of my son is like the smell of the open country.
God give you dew from heaven and the richness of the earth,
And the richness of the earth, corn and new wine in plenty!
May your mother's sons bow down to you,
A blessing on those who bless you!"

Jacob had just left when Esau came in from his hunting. He too made a tangy dish and brought it to his father.

"Come father, eat some of my tangy dish so that you may give me your blessing."

"Who are you?" asked Isaac in surprise.

"I am Esau, your eldest son," he said with equal surprise.

Isaac was confused. At first he grumbled and muttered to himself. Then he demanded in a loud voice, "Who was it that hunted and brought me venison?" When he didn't get an answer, he thundered, "I ate it all before you came in and blessed him, and the blessing must stand." He was getting very angry, and more confused.

Esau gave a loud and bitter cry. He held his head in his hands and rocked back and forth in despair. Tears filled his eyes. Then he pleaded with his father, "Bless me too."

Isaac threw the tangy dish on to the floor. He was as mad as I had ever seen him. "Your brother has tricked you out of your blessing," he screamed. And looking in my direction with a frown, he asked blankly, "What are we to do now?"

I quickly dropped my eyes and left the room. I was frightened because I thought Isaac had found me out. I was trembling.

"Have you no blessing for me?" I heard Esau whine to Isaac.

Isaac gave him a blessing, but it was not what Esau expected. The blessing included how he would serve his brother Jacob.

Now it was Esau's turn to be furious. "He tricked me! He tricked me!" he shouted at the top of his lungs. "I hate him! He better stay out of my way. I'm going to break his neck!"

I trembled. I shook. My teeth chattered. What was happening between my two sons? If Esau got hold of Jacob he would kill him. I believed him. What on earth could I do? I was desperate. Jacob must keep the blessing.

So I called Jacob aside, sat him down, and whispered in his ear, "Esau your brother is threatening to kill you. Listen to me. This is important. Slip away at once to my brother Laban. Stay with him a while until your brother's anger cools. When Esau forgets what you have done to him, I will send for you."

When the quiver and fear in my voice had settled down, I went to Isaac. He was still trembling with rage. After I had brought him some warm broth to soothe him, I told him that he should send Jacob away to my brother Laban so that he could find a proper wife. Poor Isaac. He is too old to think straight. He did call Jacob, blessed him, and sent him on his way. Thank goodness my plan worked.

Some people think I'm a cheater. Some think I betrayed my husband Isaac. But I had to work behind the scenes. God revealed to me in a dream that Jacob would carry on the family traditions.

I tricked Isaac to be sure his power of male succession didn't succeed, so that God's plan could continue. I had to do it – it was the only way.

A tale of two brothers

Although the biblical stories of brothers are usually stories of sibling rivalry, the Hebrew tradition points beyond brotherly conflict to a high ideal: "A brother is born to share troubles" (Proverbs 17:17 NEB). The following story from folklore is an illustration of such a relationship.

Many many years ago, in the land of Israel, there lived two brothers. Judah lived with his wife and children on one side of a large hill; Isaac lived alone on the other side of the hill. Each brother planted fields of wheat, barley, and oats. At the time of the harvest each would gather his grain and store it for the winter. Year after year, God blessed them both with a plentiful harvest.

One year the harvest was better than ever. The grains grew taller than the brothers could reach, golden and beautiful as far as the eye could see. Their wooden carts creaked under the weight of all this bounty.

As he was bringing in the last of his harvest, Judah thought to himself, "This is the best harvest I ever had. Certainly I have plenty of food for myself and my family. But Isaac lives all alone. My sons can help me raise more grain if we run short, but my poor brother has no one to help him. It is not right for me to enjoy this extra food. My brother deserves to have more."

That same evening, as Isaac brought in the last of his harvest, he thought, "This was a magnificent harvest. I have plenty of food for myself. But Judah has to provide for a wife and two sons. I live alone and have no one else to care for. It is not right for me to enjoy this extra food. My brother deserves to have more."

Late that night, each brother got out of bed and dressed quickly. Judah was careful not to wake his wife and children. He left his house and went outside to the pile of grain. He gathered a large part of the pile, placed it in his cart and started up the hill to bring this food to his brother's house.

Isaac also dressed quickly and gathered a large part of his grain to bring to his brother. He took a cart and started up the hill toward his brother's house.

They both reached the top of the hill at the same time and were surprised to see the other. Realizing what had happened, they jumped out of their carts and crying, they embraced.

God saw the act of brotherly love and said, "Blessed is this field where these brothers stand." God smiled. The little brooks gurgled with delight. The hills clapped their hands. The mountains roared with pleasure.

Many years later, King Solomon built the Temple on that very hill!

Adapted by permission from *Hebrew Folklore from Sidrach Stories*, ed. Steven M. Rosman, UAHC Press, New York, 1989, pp. 19-20.

Rachel

Genesis chapters 29–35, particularly Genesis 31:19 ff.

Snickering at the thought

Daughter of Laban, competitive sister of Leah, wife of Jacob – Rachel is one of the matriarchs of Israel.

The context of the particular story we are concerned with is that "Laban was not so well-disposed toward Jacob as he once had been" (Genesis 31:2). Indeed, Rachel and Leah are completely alienated from their father Laban because "he has sold us and spent on himself the whole of the money paid for us" (Genesis 31:15). They refer to the bridewealth that was given for them at the time of their marriage. Of course, their husband Jacob was not faultless either, having manipulated Laban's flocks in order to ensure ownership of the strongest animals for himself: "So Jacob increased in wealth more and more until he possessed great flocks, male and female slaves, camels and asses" (Genesis 30:43). Laban and Jacob both cheated each other whenever they could. They deserved each other.

To escape Laban's wrath, Jacob flees secretly with his wives, his livestock, and his many children to his father Isaac's home in Canaan. Before they go, Rachel steals her father's household gods.

Laban catches up with them and asks, "Why did you steal my household gods?" (Genesis 31:30). Jacob, not knowing Rachel is the culprit, protests innocence. He promises that whoever possesses the household gods will die for it, exercising his patriarchal powers of life and death over his household. Laban's search of Jacob's and Leah's tents yields nothing. Read for yourself what happened in Rachel's tent (Genesis 31:33–35).

Jacob was justifiably angry at Laban. Laban still suspected Jacob of having tricked him somehow. The two men were so suspicious of each other that they asked God to watch between them for signs of treachery. They made a pillar out of a heap of stones at Mizpah (which means Watchpost). This pillar was to be a witness between Jacob and Laban, should there be any more skullduggery on the part of either of them. The vow they made called on God to watch between them in case of more treacheries. Ironically, it is used today by Christians and known as the "Mizpah benediction": "The Lord watch between me and thee, while we are absent one from the other!" (Genesis 31:49–50).

Rachel acted in the best trickster tradition when she told Laban, "I cannot rise because the way of women is upon me"(Genesis 31:35). She was either menstruating, or pretending to. It does come in handy sometimes! Laban doesn't pursue the matter. Is it because he fears her "uncleanness"? Perhaps Rachel uses the dangerous and so-called polluting power of menstruation to deter him from discovering her theft. She undermines his male authority by exploiting what makes her distinctively female. Yet the ambiguities in Rachel's trick leave us feeling somewhat uncomfortable.

Opinions differ as to why she steals the gods. Some say that by stealing the gods, she guarantees Joseph's eventual leadership. Like Rebekah, she takes the succession of leadership into her own hands. A similar view is that the gods represent the line of descent through the mother; therefore her son Joseph would be heir to the family leadership. Maybe she believed that spiritual power and authority was bestowed on the one who possessed them. She certainly saw it as a way of bettering her sister Leah. Perhaps she was angry at her father who deceived her, and her trickery is a positive act in the context of the story. It could be that the gods were tokens of ancestor worship that may have been popular at the time.

Whatever the reasons, Rachel is later selected by Jeremiah as the mother of the nation.

For further reading

Laffey, Alice. *An Introduction to the Old Testament: a Feminist Perspective.* Fortress Press, Philadelphia, 1988.

Winter, Miriam Therese. *Woman Wisdom: Women of the Hebrew Scriptures: Part One.* Crossroad, NY, 1991.

Bellis, Alice Ogden. *Helpmates, Harlots, Heroes: Women's Stories in the Hebrew Bible.* Westminster/John Knox, Louisville, KY, 1994.

Snickering at the thought

Laban went
To Rachel's tent
To get his household gods;
When he got there
The tent was bare
He said to himself, "How odd!"

Listen to him shouting: "Where are my household gods?"

My father Laban wants to find the little images of gods and goddesses that we kept in our house. Listen to him! He is shouting now in the tents of the maidservants.

"Where are my household gods?" he shouts. "Where are my gods and goddesses?"

Listen to him shout. If he discovers I have them, I will pay with my life. But he won't find them. I have placed myself on the camel cushion, and under my skirts I hide the gods, the little images I have taken. Oh, you're probably thinking, her father will find them.

But no! You wait and see.

I'm not a robber. These clay images are mine, and I take them back again from him. My husband Jacob was cunning enough to take a blessing from his blind old father Isaac. That guaranteed he would be the leader of his people as God wished. In the same way, if I own the household gods they will stand as symbols of God's favor to me and my sons. Even if Joseph is not Jacob's firstborn, these household gods will secure his place ahead of Leah's children. It will be as though he were the first son born to Jacob. That will put Leah in her proper place. After all, I'm Jacob's beloved wife now. Shouldn't my son Joseph be chosen ahead of Leah's – she who was never truly loved?

I carry with me, hidden beneath my skirts, the hope for the future of my people, through Joseph.

Do you hear Laban? Now he is in my sister Leah's tent. "Where are my household gods?" he bellows.

Laban my father has traveled seven days to find us, for we left without his knowledge when he went to shear his sheep. And this morning I listened from my tent as he confronted my husband Jacob: "Where are my household gods? Why have you stolen my gods?"

And Jacob responded, "I haven't stolen them. Come and search. If you find them in any of our tents, that person shall die."

I believe him. My husband Jacob loves me. But he loves his own welfare and his own status more. So he will see that I am killed if the household gods are found.

Why should I risk my life for these sacred images? These little gods and goddesses I hide beneath my skirt are meaning and power for me. They remind me of the future of my ancestry and of my people. They secure the family leadership for Joseph.

But my life will be spared, and I will tell you why. In a moment my father will come to my tent. He will roar, "Where are my household gods?" He will feel all my belongings and search everywhere.

And I will say to him: "Father, forgive me, but I cannot rise before you, for the common lot of women is upon me." He knows that when that monthly time comes to every woman, she is considered unclean. No man may approach her. What nonsense! I snicker at the thought.

Still, because he believes it, it will save my life.

Tamar

Genesis 38

Hook, line, and sinker

A story for children nine and up

Tamar is one of four women listed in the genealogy of Jesus (as a son of David) in Matthew 1:3. A Canaanite foreigner, her story is told in Genesis 38. Her courageous, tricky, and unorthodox action ensured that her offspring (the sons of Judah) would constitute the tribe that would eventually be David's ancestors. Like many other biblical women, she had to use deception to achieve her ends. She had to become a mother to count in that social system.

In the Hebrew practice of Levirate marriage, when the husband died without leaving a son as heir, then the wife was to bear a child for her husband via the husband's brother. This bound the woman to a relationship with that family even after her husband's death, but it also gave her a stake in the future.

Tamar was a widow. No brother of her dead husband was able or willing to impregnate her and give her a child, her only passport to a future. She knew a great injustice was being done her by Judah, her father-in-law. So she took charge.

Tamar is remembered because of her virtue. What is her virtue? She insisted that the law be kept and the tribe be preserved. Her goal was to provide through Judah what he would not provide through his sons. In some ways she bought into the patriarchal system by propping up the Levirate arrangement. But the social plight of widows was nothing to write home about. She did what she could within the confines of that system.

She could have passively accepted her lot. Instead, she planned a way to change her situation through the culture-honored method of trickery, used by underdogs in these stories.

Was she a common prostitute? According to scholar Phyllis Bird, the word actually used means "holy woman," more courtesan than whore. Bird argues Tamar is not a common prostitute, though she shares some important characteristics with her sisters of the streets, including sexual intercourse with a stranger. She was self-respecting and modest, possibly a cult prostitute. Survival of the tribe through an heir was more important to her than her own reputation.

At the conclusion of the story, Judah confesses, "She is more in the right than I am, because I did not give her my son Shelah." Ensuring the future of the tribe and providing an heir, according to tradition, was her virtue. Producing a son overrode all questions of morality.

When her life was threatened by Judah (who, incidentally, practiced a double standard by sleeping with an unidentified woman and offering her payment), she courageously confronted him. She chose the time, the place, and the circumstances that suited her to fulfill the Levirate law. She asked for the signet, the cord, and the staff, which were symbols of royalty and hint at her role as prophet. She willingly risked her life, and risked being burned for her actions.

She is a woman of impressive audacity, initiative, and willingness to take a risk.

For further reading

Day, Peggy L., ed. *Gender and Difference in Ancient Israel.* Augsburg/Fortress, Minneapolis, 1989.

Hook, line, and sinker

Tamar was a widow,
Tamar was so smart,
Judah saw that she had made
Trickery an art.

"Perez! Zarah! Your dinner is ready."

"Oh, Mom, we aren't quite finished our game yet."

"Doesn't matter. Come at once."

The twins are enjoying their evening meal with their mother.

"Mom, at school today Enoch teased me about who my father is. Who is he anyway?"

"Yeah, Mom. All the kids think the stories about our birth are really weird. Tell us about it again."

"Well," said Tamar, their mother, "your father is Judah, as you know. His wife was a foreigner, a Canaanite woman. He had three sons whose names were Er, Onan, and Shelah. According to the custom, he arranged for his oldest son Er to marry me. But Er died suddenly. The Jewish law said that Judah then had to marry me to his second son, Onan. But Onan didn't want to marry me. It turned out he didn't have to, because he too dropped dead."

"Not a good record for you, Mom," piped up Perez.

"Not good at all, Mom," echoed Zarah.

"You're right," agreed Tamar. "And Judah thought the same thing. He was scared to marry me to his remaining son Shelah, as the law required, for fear he might lose him too."

"You mean, that maybe he would also drop dead?" asked Perez.

"Exactly," said Tamar. "So he sent me home to my father, unmarried and without a child. No worse fate could fall on a woman. He promised that sometime in the future he would get Shelah to marry me. I was ashamed to go home, without a husband, and without a child. To be a widow, without a husband, was to be treated like dirt. I couldn't even leave the house by myself. There was no man to go with me. No one talked to me. I had no friends. Even my mother and father didn't really want me at home. They wanted to know why I wasn't married and why I hadn't yet had a child who would carry on the family name and inherit property. A child was the promise of a future for them."

"But you had us, Mom," said Zarah. "How come?"

"Well, the law was that a brother of my first husband had to marry me and produce a child. But Judah refused to obey the law. So I decided to think up some way I could have a special child that would please Judah and secure his name and property for the future. I knew I might have to use some trickery to do that, but that didn't scare me. In fact, I thought it might be fun!

"After Judah's wife died, I heard he was going up to Timnah to shear his sheep. I knew he would be lonely. That was my chance.

"I took off my dark widow's clothes, put a veil over my face, spilled perfume generously over myself, put on the clothes of a woman of the temple – a priestess – and waited at a fork in the road. Sure enough, Judah came along. He gave me the eye, thinking I was a common woman of the streets. Then he said, 'Let me lie with you.' The veil should have tipped him off that I was not a common prostitute, but he didn't understand that. I bargained with him. It was risky, but fun! I asked for the usual fee of a kid from his flock of sheep. I also asked him for a pledge, until he sent the kid. I really had to flirt a lot to get his agreement. I asked for his seal, his cord, and the staff he held in his hand – all symbols of royalty. I planned on using these later to identify him as the father of the child I hoped to conceive by him.

"Did he fall for your trick?" asked Perez.

"Hook, line and sinker," Tamar replied. "I spent the night with him, and then went back to my father's house and put on my dark widow's clothes again. Nobody was the wiser."

"Then what happened?" Zarah wanted to know.

"Judah sent a friend with the kid, hoping to get back the ring, the cord and the staff, but he couldn't find the woman he had slept with. Of course he couldn't – what a dummy! He had no idea the trap I had set for him. No one knew where the temple woman had gone. Judah didn't make a fuss about getting his ring and cord and staff back, probably because he was afraid of being laughed at publicly. Besides, he might get a bad name if he made a stink.

"About three months later, some people told Judah that I was pregnant, without a husband. What shame that would bring on him and his family! So he ordered that I be burned. He had no idea **he** was the father! So I sent word to him,"By the man to whom these belong, I am with child. Mark whose these are: the signet, the cord and the staff." I could hardly wait to see his reaction. He wouldn't be burning me when the truth came out – of that I was sure.

"When I was hauled up before him, he eventually had to claim the ring, the cord and the staff as **his**. Judah's face was so red I thought it would burst into flame. **Everyone** knew they were his. He took some time examining each object in detail, pretending to decide whether or not it was his. He turned the ring over five times, slipping it on his little finger to prove it was too big, but finally having to put it on his third finger. It fitted! He couldn't deny what had happened. He couldn't deny he was the father of my child.

"To his credit (or maybe just because he saw he was trapped) Judah knelt down, wept a little, and blurted out, 'Tamar is right.

She did the right thing. In refusing to give her my third son Shelah I broke the law of our people. She knew she would have to do whatever she could to ensure the permanence of my tribe and its future. What am I without a son to follow me? Nothing.'

"The rest you know. When you were born, I was recognized as part of Judah's family. After all, he was nothing without me, and he knew it."

"Did our father ever forgive you for tricking him? Was he mad at you a long time?" asked Perez.

"Yeah," said Zarah, "how long was it before he trusted you again?"

Tamar laughed. "When he saw how beautiful you both were, and that you were boys who would carry his name in history, he forgave me. Did he trust me after that? He certainly did! In fact, any time he had a trick to play on someone, he always asked me first how to do it!"

Determined Delilah

Judges 16

Prying open Samson's secret

For children age seven and up

Who hasn't heard of Delilah? Even today, it's an insult to be called "a Delilah" (or a Philistine!). Who was this woman?

The Samson stories are more legendary than any other material in the book of Judges. They emerged shortly after 1200 BCE when the Philistines (not a Semitic people) with their superior skill in weapons of iron, came close to making Canaan a Philistine empire. "Philistine" is an archaic variant of "Palestinian," and one of the great ironies of history is that the name later given to Israel's land, Palestine, is derived from the name of Israel's archenemies, the Philistines! The land was semi-occupied by a hostile army, as many countries involved in civil war are today, and it was most unclear as to which side was on top. The Book of Judges is filled with stories of wars and clashes and of local or regional leaders – like Samson, Gideon, Jephthah, and Deborah – who temporarily unified the people and saved the Israelites from defeat and extinction.

Samson, a kind of jock football-hero type, was a man of immense physical strength. The Philistine lords called on one of their own, Delilah, to betray him into their hands (verse 6), offering money. Did she do it for her national pride, or just for the money? All we know is she played hardball, and must have felt somewhat confident of her success.

The story goes that Samson loved her. Delilah asked Samson the source of his strength and he lied to her, not once but three times (Judges 16:13–14). Delilah then taunted him with his protestations of love. How could he treat her this way (verse 15)? Finally he told her the truth and she was able to deliver him into the hands of the Philistine lords who were close by (16:15–21).

Traditionally, Delilah has been portrayed as deceitful, dangerous, treacherous, and sexually seductive – in contrast to Samson, who is portrayed as an Israelite Tarzan, a Hebrew superhero. Renaissance art and popular music contribute to the understanding of Delilah as a temptress, second only to Eve.

A close reading of the text, however, calls these interpretations into question. Her action may have been a courageous act of national loyalty, as well as the action of a trickster, since she knew Samson to be responsible for the deaths of thousands of her Philistine people. Perhaps she was motivated by the offer of a large sum of money. And while she may have betrayed her "lover" to the Philistines, at least she was honest. She never once professed love for him.

We should, at the very least, try to read the story from her perspective. How may she have felt about a man who said he loved her, but then told her lies, not once, but three times? How may she have felt about a man who broke his Nazirite vow (Judges 13:3–5) when he ate the honey from the carcass of a dead lion (14:9)? How may she have felt about a man torturing animals (15:4–5)? What about Samson's failed marriage, and the horrible events that led to his wife being burned to death as a result of his actions (14:1–15:8)? What about his enjoyment of a prostitute (16:1) before settling on Delilah?

How has this man been turned into a popular hero?

Samson is usually portrayed as an innocent victim, though he treated everyone – including Delilah – as an object and used any means to achieve his ends. He knew what was going on in his relationship with Delilah and was an active participant in events, not merely a victim.

My story focuses, not on Delilah's seductive wiles, but on her wit, resourcefulness, trickery, persistence, and her act of national loyalty. She is a woman who took care of herself, and her identity was not bound to any man. The patriarchal bias of the biblical story requires some openness to this alternate interpretation.

For further reading

Laffey, Alice. *An Introduction to the Old Testament: a Feminist Perspective.* Fortress Press, Philadelphia, 1988.

Bellis, Alice Ogden. *Helpmates, Harlots, Heroes: Women's Stories in the Hebrew Bible.* Westminster/John Knox Press, Louisville, KY, 1994, pp. 124 ff.

Prying open Samson's secret

"Tell me, tell me, tell me."
"I won't, I can't," he said.
"Tell me, tell me, tell me."
One day she shaved his head.

"I have never loved anyone but you, Delilah," whispered Samson in her ear. He pulled her toward him on the silk-covered pile of rugs in the corner of her comfortable house. "I love you, Delilah."

She laughed and freed herself. Samson frowned. "Why do you laugh?" he asked.

"Because, Samson. Because you really think you love me more than all the others. More than your former wife. More than that prostitute you had sex with. I know all about your former love life, you know. And here you are betraying your own people by consorting with me, a woman of the Philistines, the sworn enemies of your people."

Samson adored her. Delilah was so good to him. She peeled his grapes and always kept a large supply of his favorite foods on hand.

"Delilah. Delilah. My life is an open book. I really do love you."

She was silent. For some time, she made no response. Then she began to play a game with not-so-clever Samson. He loved the game because it was all about him.

She stood up. "If you really loved me, you would tell me the secret of your strength. From what I've heard, nothing on earth can bind you because you have the strength of ten. You are not like other men of Israel. You can uproot a tree with one hand and break bricks with the other. And once, when you were furious, you killed a thousand Philistines with only the jawbone of an ass as your weapon."

Now Delilah was not an Israelite. Her people, the Philistines, were enemies of Israel. She had been offered a lot of money by each Philistine ruler if she could discover the secret of Samson's strength. Then they could destroy him, and her people, the Philistines, would triumph. So she kept asking:

"Tell me, tell me, tell me."
"I won't, I can't," he said.
"Tell me, tell me, tell me."
But Samson shook his head.

Samson laughed. "You want to know the secret of my strength? Is that all that worries you? If I tell you, will it prove I love you? All right. I'll tell you. If you bind me with seven fresh bow strings – still green and strong – then I become weak like other men."

She clapped her hands, and a Philistine ruler who had been lying in wait in a nearby room brought the fresh bow strings immediately. Delilah tied the laughing Samson tightly and then cried,

"The Philistines are upon you, Samson!"

Samson, thinking it was a silly little game, snapped the bow strings as easily as a strand of fiber snaps when it touches the fire. Samson reached laughingly for Delilah and asked for a kiss.

Once more she begged to know the secret of his strength:

"Tell me, tell me, tell me."
"I won't, I can't," he said.
"Tell me, tell me, tell me."
Still Samson shook his head.

He told her, "If they bind me with new ropes that have never been used I shall become weak like other men."

So Delilah took the new ropes and tied him up.

Then she cried, "The Philistines are upon you, Samson."

Again he snapped the new ropes as though they were thread. Delilah laughed with him, pretending it was a lover's game. But she began to understand it was time to play for real. She was not an Israelite. In her heart, she wanted the Philistines to rule the people of Israel. Besides, she wanted the money that had been promised her by the Philistine rulers. Samson was a big man, but even bigger money had been offered to her.

Samson continued to visit her. He thought of no one else but her night and day.

"Samson," she murmured, "are you trying to make a fool of me with your lies and games? How can I know you really love me? Tell me the secret of your strength." Her face was close to his, but she was frowning:

"Tell me, tell me, tell me."
"I won't, I can't," he said.
"Tell me, tell me, tell me."
And still he shook his head.

He said, "This time, Delilah, I will certainly tell you the truth. Weave the seven locks of my hair into that cloth you're weaving on your loom, and I'll be as helpless as a bird caught in a snare."

She was sure this was his secret. Cradling his big head in her arms, she lulled him to sleep. Then after she had deftly woven the locks of his long hair into the cloth on her loom she shouted, " The

Philistines are upon you, Samson!"

He leaped up, tearing his hair from the loom and breaking the loom into pieces.

"Samson," she protested, "how can you say you love me when you never tell me the truth? Three times you have lied to me. You have not told me what gives you such great strength."

She was determined to gain the victory for her people. Day after day she pestered him with the same words: "Samson, if you love me, tell me your secret."

"I can't, I can't," he said.

"Tell me, tell me, tell me."
"I won't, I can't," he said.
"Tell me, tell me, tell me."
One day she shaved his head.

Because Samson wasn't having any fun at all. He grew tired of her nagging. And so he broke his vow to God. He told his secret to the woman who had done what a thousand Philistine warriors had not been able to do.

"No razor has touched my head," he said, "because I am a Nazirite consecrated to God from the day of my birth. If my hair were cut then my strength would leave me, and I would be as weak as any other man."

Delilah told no one at first. She was sure that Samson had not lied to her this time. But nothing must go wrong. She stayed close to him for some time. She sent for the Philistine lords secretly and said, "He has told me his secret." So they brought her the money.

When she had lulled Samson asleep on her knees, she signaled the Philistine rulers who were lying in wait in the nearby room and their razors flashed. Delilah could feel the strength leave Samson's strong arms and shoulders.

"The Philistines are upon you, Samson!" she cried.

He awakened at once and stood up. "I will go out as usual," he thought to himself, not knowing his strength had left him. And not knowing that even Delilah could control him now.

The shrewd woman of Tekoah

2 Samuel 14:1–24

Flattery never fails

This story is usually called "The Wise Woman of Tekoah." I think rather, it should be "The Shrewd Woman of Tekoah."

The story starts with the rape of Tamar by her half brother Amnon and the revenge taken against Amnon by Tamar's full brother Absalom. (Don't confuse this Tamar with the Tamar who was an ancestor of King David in Genesis 38. Tamar was a relatively common name of that time, much like Anne or Joan in our time.) After the rape became known, Absalom murdered his brother Amnon, who was also David's eldest son and presumed heir. So it was a struggle for power in David's family, as well as filial revenge. Although David had other sons, Absalom was now in the strongest position to make a bid for the leadership of the kingdom. Recognizing the threat, King David expelled his son Absalom for three years. But Joab, David's top general, worried about the kingdom's dissolution if civil war over succession broke out. Joab saw Absalom as the best future hope for king. And doubtless he himself stood to gain by Absalom's return.

At the instigation of Joab, who saw "the king's heart was set on Absalom," an unnamed woman became a major player to guarantee Absalom's return. Joab selected her to tell David a story intended to convince him to let Absalom back into his good graces.

The woman was to dress and act like a widow. She was to tell the king she had two sons but now had only one, since one had killed the other. The dead son's relatives (by marriage, presumably) called for vengeance and wanted to kill the surviving son. But if that happened, she would be stripped of her identity and her husband's name would cease to exist in Israel.

The parallel, of course, was that David's continuing exile of Absalom spelled nothing but disaster for the kingdom.

The story takes for granted that a dead man needed a living son to keep his name alive in Israel. The widow, who pretends she is about to lose her son, knows this, and therefore ahead of all other considerations, places primary importance on keeping her son alive. Her earnest pleas are met with a positive response, "Not a hair of your son's head shall fall to the ground," says David.

"How then could it enter your head to do this same wrong to God's people," she cunningly asks him, convincing him that the entire nation will suffer if the royal family breaks up. She counsels the King that vengeance should take a secondary place to the preservation of the life of his son, and therefore, of the kingdom.

Through combined references to guilt and sin, goodness and wisdom, she shrewdly manipulates the king to measure up to his public image, ignoring the damning details of his private life. Even when David detects the fine hand of Joab manipulating this script, the widow freely admits to it – and shrewdly offers even greater flattery about David's wisdom. She astutely coerces the king while keeping her own self safe. It was not a minor accomplishment for a woman in her position, given the context.

David does take her advice. He recalls Absalom from exile, but because he has not really been convinced of the rightness of his decision, he does not welcome Absalom into his presence. Absalom's return leads to his bid for the kingdom and eventually, to his death.

For further reading

Bellis, Agnes Ogden. *Helpmates, Harlots, Heroes: Women's Stories in the Hebrew Bible.* Westminster/John Knox, 1994, pp. 140 ff.

Williams, Michael. *The Storyteller's Companion to the Bible*, Vol. IV. Abingdon, Nashville, 1993, pp. 135 ff.

Flattery never fails

They call me wise,
They call me shrewd,
I don't tell lies,
I catch the king's mood.

I was summoned by Joab.

Joab told me: "King David's son Absalom has been in exile for three years. He fled after killing his brother Amnon for a great crime he had committed, and David has not yet forgiven him. I know, however, that David's heart is set on Absalom. I hope they may be reconciled. I have a proposal for you."

I knew Joab wanted to curry David's favor, because his own

career depended on it. And I suppose he thought the way to David's heart was through his loved son Absalom. But I wondered what on earth Joab's proposal could be. And why me?

"I want you to pretend to be in mourning for the dead. Do not anoint yourself with oil or perfume. Be like a woman who has lost a husband and is grieving. Wear black clothing," he said.

It sounded fine so far. What else did he want?

"Then go to King David and repeat what I tell you. I will tell you exactly what to say."

That part wasn't so good. I was willing to hear his proposal, but I will decide myself what I am going to say. No man is going to write a script for me. It's not for nothing I am known as a "shrewd woman."

Joab would go with me to the king's court.

When I came into the king's presence, I threw myself face downwards on the ground, and cried, "Help, your majesty!"

The king asked, "What is it?"

I answered, "Sir, I am a widow. My husband is dead. I had two sons. They came to blows out in the country where there was no one to part them, and one of them struck the other and killed him. Now sir, my in-laws all have risen against me. They cry, 'Hand over the man who killed his brother, so that we can put him to death for taking his brother's life, and so obey the law.' If they do this, they will cut off my last hope and leave my husband no name and no descendant on earth."

"Go home," said the king, "and I will settle your case."

But I didn't go home. Instead I continued, "Let the guilt be on me, your majesty, and on my father's house; let the king and his throne be blameless." I thought that would help him decide what to do.

Sure enough, the king said to me, "If anyone says anything more to you, bring him to me and he will never bother you again."

Then I started again, "Let your majesty call upon the Lord your God, to prevent his brothers bound on vengeance from doing their worst and destroying my son." I thought calling on God wouldn't hurt either.

The king swore, "As the Lord lives, not a hair of your son's head shall fall to the ground."

Then I thought, I want to plead that he show mercy to his son. I want to beg that they stop being at each other's throats. I am so sick and tired of men fighting and killing and wanting vengeance, when what is needed is family unity. So I said, "May I add one more word, your majesty?"

"Say on," sighed the king.

I screwed up my courage and continued, "How then could it enter your head to do this same wrong to God's people? Out of your own mouth, your majesty, you condemn yourself. You have refused to bring back the man you have banished." (I meant Absalom but I didn't dare use the name openly.) "We shall all die. We shall be like water that is spilt on the ground and lost; but God will spare the man who does not set himself to keep the outlaw in exile."

The king looked furious. He didn't like being told what to do by a mere woman. So I thought I had better provide some excuses for myself. "I came to say this to you, your majesty, because the people have threatened me. I thought to myself, 'If only I can speak to the king, perhaps he will pay attention to my words; he will listen and he will save me from the man who is seeking to cut off me and my son together from Israel, God's own possession.' I thought too that the words of my Lord the king would be a comfort to me; for your majesty is like the angel of God and can decide between right and wrong." (Joab gave me some of the other words, but I thought up that bit about being like an angel. It's true he has the power to decide right from wrong, but this king is no angel! The details of his private life are well known in the kingdom – particularly how he treated Bathsheba, Abigail, and Michal.)

"The Lord your God be with you," I added piously.

Then the king said to me, "Don't tell me any lies. Now I ask **you** a question."

"Speak, your majesty," I said, my knees quivering.

"Did Joab tell you what to say?" he asked.

There was no way around it. "Yes, your majesty. Yes, your servant Joab did prompt me. He put the story into my mouth. He did it to give a new turn to this affair." (That was a hidden way of saying it was time the men stopped slaughtering each other, and the royal family became a unity once more.) "Your majesty is as wise as an angel of God and knows all that goes on in the land." (I thought it worth repeating that he is as wise as an angel. Flattery usually works.)

The king said to Joab, "You have my consent. Go and fetch back the young man Absalom, my son." (I knew all along that is what David really wanted, because Absalom was his favorite son.) Joab knelt before the king and then left the court to find Absalom and have him return to Jerusalem.

I backed out of the court, smiling to myself. Even kings can be wheedled into doing certain things if you know the words they want to hear – like "wise" and "angel."

I almost burst out laughing. If there was anything David was **not**, it was wise and angelic. Too bad I couldn't have been his adviser way back. He would have done so much better if I'd been around!

Women of the early church

Lydia

Acts 16:9–15 and Acts 4:32–37

The foul smell of fine clothing

Lydia was the first convert to Christianity on the European continent. We are not sure if she was wealthy or not, although in Christian circles she is usually described as a successful businesswoman who had her own household. German theologian Luise Schottroff suggests she may have been in the dirty business of tanning, producing the purple cloths herself. The dye industries were located outside the urban zone because no one could stand the smell. Lydia was born and raised in a similar dye industrial ghetto outside the city of Thyatira. There, she was probably a textile worker, paid next to starvation wages. The only people who wore the purple fabric she made were the top people at court.

She moved on to the big foreign city of Philippi to find a better job, as many other women in the Roman Empire had to do. But even in Philippi she found herself once again outside the city limits, working alongside other women who worked there. She was certainly an "outcast" because of her trade, and may well have been poor in her beginnings, which she never forgot.

However, she prospered as an independent woman and became an influential one, able to decide for herself whether to become a Christian, and to decide for her household. She must have been self-confident and intelligent – how otherwise could she have been a "dealer in fabric"?

She met other women regularly outside the city by the riverside. It was a place for stillness, meditation, prayer. She was a "worshiper of God" and listened intently to Paul. What did he tell her? That in Jesus Christ all distinctions between rich and poor, male and female, Jew and Greek were at an end? Surely this was somewhat dangerous for Lydia, a businesswoman in the trade of marketing purple fabrics to the wealthy. She would need to remember who her customers were, and to remember that they did not consider her their social equal! She would need to avoid undermining the system.

Acts 16:9–11 indicates that she invited Paul and Barnabas to stay at her house in Philippi. So she must have been a woman in high standing with the earliest Christian communities. Her invitation does not necessarily indicate she was prosperous enough to have a huge house. Many of limited means are extremely hospitable in opening up their homes. Lydia was used to doing this, as the church met in her house in Philippi.

Maybe they sat on the floor! I wonder if in her house church "everything was held in common" (Acts 4:33).

What follows is an imaginative reconstruction of her story.

For further reading

Robins, Wendy S. and Musimbi R.A. Kanyoro. *Speaking for Ourselves.*, WCC, Geneva, 1990, pp. 39, 59, and 91–94.

The foul smell of fine clothing

She's poor but shrewd.
She stands so tall.
She changed her life.
'Twas due to Paul.

Dear Lydia,

My mom says you worked in leather and purple dyes. My mom sometimes works in leather. It stinks. When she comes home from work to our three rooms over a storefront, I have to hold my nose. Are your hands always wrinkled, chapped, and stained like hers? Do you often get sick at your stomach with the smell?

We live in downtown Toronto on Spadina Ave. We might as well live miles outside the city as you did, we feel so separate from the rest of the city. My mom works mostly in rich textiles or leathers which only the wealthy people can afford to buy. Same as only the top people at the court got to wear the purple fabric you made.

Most of the women Mom works with come from other countries, and are different from us. But you know something about that, don't you? You were a Gentile who lived among Jews and

Phoenicians. Were you attracted to the Jews by their good morals? I bet you learned a thing or two about making purple dye from the Phoenician women.

Some of the women here are Asians, some Filipino, some black. But they're pretty well all women. The only thing they have in common is that they have no voice, no power, no influence. You know all about that too, don't you? Most of the people who worked with you were like that too. They were women, they were alone, and they didn't count.

For long long hours every day Mom gets paid just about zip. Sometimes she gets paid only piecework – that means, so much money for every jacket she sews. We fill up on bread and Kraft dinner. Sometimes we get to have a dented can of tuna. But you know all about that too.

We moved to Toronto from a small town in Europe, thinking things would be better here. Such a long way! But you moved from Asia Minor to Macedonia, didn't you? Such a long way! You moved from a small place too, and traveled a long way to the big seaside city of Philippi. I suppose that was so you could make use of the sea's shellfish to make more exquisite purple dye.

It wasn't any better for you at first either, was it? You still worked at a place outside the city limits. But somehow you managed to become a business woman and trade in purple fabric. Good for you! It must have taken a lot of hard work to become wealthy, and you did it without a husband too. Did the Businesswomen's Club ask you to join? Or did your chapped hands still count against you? Mom's factory isn't outside the city limits so maybe she'll meet some of the rich women who used to live in Spadina Ave.'s textile district or in Kensington Market where the raw meat hangs from hooks. They live up on the hill now, and they're wealthy, believe me!

You went a lot to a peaceful place beside the river, didn't you? That's where you met Paul. What did he say to you? Did he tell you about the equality of women and men in Jesus? Or did he tell you to be silent in the church, and to ask your husband at home if you had any questions? But you're not married, so how could you? And you're the leader of a house church. How could you possibly not speak? I can't figure Paul out sometimes.

But **you** must have liked what he said because you asked him to baptize you and all your household! Then you invited him and his friend to stay with you at your house. It sure must have been crowded when you opened up your house to newly baptized Christians. Write and tell me what it was like. We often go near the lakeside here, but it's hard to find a quiet spot.

Your friend,
Maria.

Prisca

1 Corinthians 16:19, Rom. 16:1–5, 2 Tim. 4:19,
and Acts 18:2–4 and 26.

Friends in the right places

Romans 16 mentions the names of 26 colleagues of Paul. Ten are women. Many, like Priscilla, were leaders of their own house communities. Their influence extended from Caesarea to Rome. Mothers, sisters, wives, and young girls worked at spreading the news and building up the communities. Their functions were wide ranging. They traveled as missionaries; they preached, taught, and gathered believers together. There were well-to-do women among them as well as poor women and slaves.

Priscilla, known in the diminutive as Prisca, was one such eminent missionary who related to some of the earliest "house churches," notably those in Corinth (1 Corinthians 16:19), Rome (1 Corinthians 16:5), and Ephesus (Acts 18:18). Since her name is mentioned before her husband's four times out of six, we conclude she may have been a leading figure. Although Luke concentrates on the great missionary Paul, his remarks about these women leaders indicate that he and his sources probably knew more about them than he relates.

Priscilla and Aquila supported themselves by their secular trade, as did Paul. They were probably married. According to theologian Elisabeth Schussler Fiorenza, the early Christian house churches were not patterned after patriarchal household structures, but more on a basis of mutuality.

Prisca taught Apollos, a cultured Jew from Alexandria who became one of the earliest missionaries. Baptized by John the Baptist, he knew the teachings of Jesus, and was "instructed accurately in the way of God" by Prisca (Acts 18:26).

American theologian Bernadette Brooten, having researched the position of women in the early synagogues, found that there existed a number of women leaders. They emerged and came to the Jesus movement because they already questioned their own culture. Jesus awakened, supported, and strengthened their desire for liberation. Priscilla was one of these.

Christian apologists in the second century played down the role of women in the Christian community to avoid being ridiculed for belonging to an effeminate religion, according to Elisabeth Schussler Fiorenza. There is also evidence that early Christian leaders wrote against other Christian groups (such as the Gnostics) who accorded women a greater role in the life and preaching of the Christian community. Most of the genuine "herstory" is therefore lost. The few surviving traces have to be re-imagined as I have done here with Priscilla.

The structure erected to house the image of Diana (also known by her Greek name Artemis), the patron goddess of Ephesus, was one of the seven wonders of the ancient world. It attracted visitors from all over the Roman empire.

In this story, I have used the name Diana, as it appears in four out of the six Bible translations I consulted. The NRSV uses the name Artemis, but I think Diana is easier for children.

The cult of Diana was a major tourist industry. Pilgrims to the shrine had to be housed and fed. They deposited treasures in the temple chambers, and bought souvenir replicas of the shrine to take home with them.

However, there had been a marked decline in tourist revenues since Paul started preaching in Ephesus. The manufacturers and artisans of the souvenirs lead the opposition to Paul. The riot took place in the amphitheater before the town assembly. Ruins of this theater are still visible today in the marshy remains of Ephesus. In Paul's time, this theater seated 25,000 people – which gives some idea of the commercial importance, in those days, of both the cult of Diana and the city of Ephesus.

The man Alexander, who was put forward by the Jews in the story to try to speak to the crowd, was shouted down when they realized he was a Jew. Here is evidence that the early Christians based their work in the Jewish synagogues, and most converts came out of the Jewish community.

For further reading

Brooten, Bernadette J. *Women Leaders in the Ancient Synagogue.* Scholars Press, Chico, CA, 1982.

Fiorenza, Elisabeth Schussler. *But She Said.* Beacon Press, Boston, 1992.

Heine, Susanne. *Women and Early Christianity: A Reappraisal.* Augsburg/Fortress, Minneapolis, 1988.

Friends in the right places

"Run the people of The Way
Right out of town," they roared, "Hey, hey!"
Priscilla helped to end the riot;
I like her way – you oughta try it.

I hung around Priscilla's house a lot. She was such a neat lady! She had come to Ephesus some time ago. My family and I went to the church in her house for worship. She used me as a messenger. She always told me what was in the written note I was to deliver for her – so there were no secrets. That was so neat. She treated me like a grownup, not like a nuisance kid.

This one day she called me in, and read me a note that I was to deliver to one of the women leaders at the Temple of Diana.

"Perhaps you remember meeting me in the market place. I think we were both buying grapes for dessert. I have been in Ephesus for some time now, and would really like to talk with you. As I told you, I do not worship Diana the goddess, as I am a Christian. But I know you are a leader in her temple. There are very few women leaders in any religious community, and I think we might have a lot in common. Will you come to see me tomorrow at four o'clock?"

The woman leader of the Temple of Diana arrived promptly at four. Aquila – that's Priscilla's man – made himself scarce as men do when women talk. I hung around, since I had nothing better to do, and usually the conversation was fun.

"I fled Emperor Claudius' persecution of Christians in Rome, and came here," Priscilla was saying. She showed her new friend the tents she and Aquila were stitching.

"That's how we support ourselves," she explained to her guest. "Our friend Paul does the same thing. He's been back here in Ephesus for two years now. But it's the confusion and anger in the city that I want to talk to you about."

That's when I became all ears. I knew that many people were converting to the Christian cause. "The Way," it was called. The change had raised a lot of opposition in the city. Paul's preaching had convinced some people who used to practice magic to burn their books publicly. Now the booksellers were losing business. Ephesus was the guardian of the great goddess Diana, and didn't welcome the small upstart Christian community. Nobody paid attention to a small 11 year-old girl like me, so I heard plenty in the shops and market.

"It's not your fault that silver-tongued Apollos speaks so well that people flock to your cause," said Priscilla's guest. "None of your people have stolen anything from the temple, and you've not preached disrespect of our goddess."

"I'm glad to hear you say that," responded Priscilla. "I'm happy we have a bond of friendship and understanding between us. Maybe we can prevent the men from blowing things sky high."

Two days later, the storm broke. Demetrius, the silversmith, earned his living by making silver shrines and pendants of Diana. He had a big business going and was getting rich. I heard he was gathering his craftsmen together with men in similar work. So I hung out and listened. As usual, nobody noticed me.

"Men," he said, "you all realize your jobs depend on selling our silver work to the worshippers of Diana. If you open your ears and use your eyes, you'll know that Paul and his friends have changed the minds of a lot of people here in Ephesus. They've been telling them that our silver shrines and pendants are not gods at all!"

Ee-ee-ee—k! If that was what Paul was saying, how on earth could Priscilla keep her friendship with anyone from the temple? I wanted to run and tell her what was going on, but Demetrius was still talking. He was some talker!

"Now the danger is not only that our work might fall off, but that the temple of Diana herself might get weaker and weaker. Fewer people would come. There is even a further danger – that fewer people will worship her in Asia, and indeed in the whole world!"

What a windbag! Trying to save his own skin by scaring them that their goddess Diana would not be honored anywhere in the whole world. When what he really meant was, "You'll lose your jobs if Diana doesn't provide us with an endless supply of suckers."

When they heard Demetrius, the ringleaders all jeered:

"Run the people of the The Way
Right out of town – hey, hey!"

When the silversmiths heard Demetrius, they got furious. They cursed and yelled.

"Great is Diana of the Ephesians," the cheerleader shrieked.

"Great is Diana of the Ephesians," the workers screamed.

"Great is Diana of the Ephesians," the market vendors yelled.

The chant spread. Even people who had nothing to do with Diana, or with the silver trade, were shouting it. Soon the whole city was in an uproar.

And the ringleaders led the chorus of anger:

"Run the people of the The Way
Right out of town – hey, hey!"

I couldn't find my way back to Priscilla's house because the roads were blocked with surging crowds. Men had grabbed sticks and women had filled their skirts with stones. I was scared. I saw a woman who had fallen. Her face was all bloody, but no one seemed to care. There was shouting and pushing.

"Run the people of the The Way
Right out of town – hey, hey!"

"Those troublemakers don't belong here," I heard one man shout as he hurled a stick at nobody in particular. Most had no idea why they had come together in such a crowd. I was so small I was afraid of being crushed, so I climbed a tree.

I heard later that Paul himself wanted to speak to the crowd, but his friends wouldn't let him. It was too dangerous.

I saw a man whose name I knew was Alexander, whom the Jews put forward, pushed to the front of the crowd. He tried to quiet the crowd. He started to make a speech of defense to the people. But as soon as they discovered he was a Jew they shouted as one person, "Great is Diana of the Ephesians!" The screaming and shouting went on and on.

"Run the people of the The Way
Right out of town – hey, hey!"

The chant was like a mighty wave, crashing against a cliff.

I had spied a way back to Priscilla's house from my tree top perch. So I clambered down, sneaked around and through the crowd, and finally reached her house. What a relief to find her at home.

"What's happening?" she quizzed me anxiously, giving me a big hug. "I was afraid you had been hurt in the riot downtown."

I told her what I had heard and seen. She immediately called Aquila and told him she was going to do what she could to keep Paul out of the spotlight. It was dangerous for her to venture out, but she was determined. Aquila was not to worry – she would watch herself. She hoped her friend in Diana's Temple could speak to the ringleaders of the riot and bring some order to the city. Possibly she might have some influence with the city clerk.

I decided to go back to my tree top. It was a nice safe place and it gave me a great view of everything! The crowd was still shouting:

"Run the people of the The Way
Right out of town – hey, hey!"

Priscilla's friend must have done her work well. The town clerk jumped up on a platform and tried to quiet the crowd.

But the ringleaders started up their chant again: "Great is Diana of the Ephesians!"

The words echoed off the walls and buildings: "Great is Diana of the Ephesians!"

The town clerk raised both his arms, palms down, as he gestured to the crowd to be silent.

"Give him a chance. He's one of us," called a firm voice from the crowd.

"Let's hear what he has to say," shouted another.

The town clerk urged them everyone to be calm. "These followers of The Way haven't stolen from our temple. Nor have they shown disrespect for our goddess Diana," he asserted. His words echoed exactly what I had heard in Priscilla's sitting room.

"What about our jobs?" roared one man.

"I have to support my family," shouted another.

And the silence became a whispering, and the whispering became a muttering, and the muttering became a babbling, and the babbling became a shouting, and the shouting became a mighty roar like a huge waterfall smashing against the rocks.

"Run the people of the The Way
Right out of town – hey, hey!"

The town clerk raised his arms again, palms down, and gestured for silence. Slowly the roaring quieted to a shouting. The shouting became a babbling. The babbling became a muttering. The muttering became a murmuring. And the murmuring died away to a whisper. And then there was silence again.

He turned to Demetrius, the main rabble-rouser.

"Demetrius, if you or any of your fellow workers have a charge to bring against anyone, take it to the law courts. We better be careful or we'll all be charged with rioting by the Romans. We have no excuse for the commotion we've made."

The men dropped their sticks. The women let their stones fall to the ground. As suddenly as it had started, the riot was over.

"Now," the town clerk said, "let's all go home."

They all did. They went slowly at first, muttering and grumbling to each other. But they went.

I slid down my tree. Dodging the elbows and squeezing through wall-to-wall people, made my way back to Priscilla's house. What a good piece of work she had done today, I thought.

What a neat lady!

Rhoda

Acts 12:12–17

Nobody believed her

The mention in Acts 11:19 of the "scattering abroad" of the members of the Christian community marks a turning point in Christian history. Official opposition, including open persecution, began against the growing influence of Christians. Herod Agrippa, grandson of Herod the Great, through political maneuvering with Rome, had himself declared ruler of nearly all the regions once ruled by his grandfather. He sought to curry favor with Jewish leaders to consolidate his power.

This is reflected in the story in Acts 12:1–13. The popular acclaim that he received after he had executed James, the son of Zebedee, led Agrippa to imprison Peter too.

A slave girl named Rhoda plays a significant role in that story. She belonged to the community of Mary, the mother of John Mark, in Jerusalem. She must have been integrated into the community life of that early Christian group for some time, because she recognized Peter by his voice.

The text pictures a situation where Rhoda was taking part in the community's meeting, doubtless by leave of the owner. She was one of those who (as in Acts 2:42) devoted herself to praying, eating, and praising God. When someone knocked at the door in the middle of the night, she went to it. She recognized the voice of Peter who was known to be in prison. Realizing that a miracle had taken place, she didn't open the door, but rather ran back to spread the good news.

Nobody believed her. "You're out of your mind," they said. But she persisted. Interestingly, it is the same verb, "persisted," that Luke's story (Luke 22:59) uses for the female slave who unmasked Peter, in the high priest's courtyard, just before he denied Jesus. In this story, though, Peter keeps on knocking.

Finally, the group went to the door to check out the slave girl's story. And they were overjoyed by the miracle of Peter's liberation.

The community's disbelief has nothing to do with Rhoda being a slave, and everything to do with her being female. It parallels the male disciple's disbelief in the female disciples' story of Jesus' resurrection (Luke 24:11). In both instances, the women persist in their belief in God's power, despite the community's scorn and disbelief.

The slave girl's self-assertiveness, and her trust in God's power, are the core of this story.

For further reading

Schottroff, Luise. *Lydia's Impatient Sisters: a Feminist Social History of Early Christianity.* Westminster/John Knox Press, Louisville, KY, 1995.

Nobody believed her

I knew it was him
Though they wouldn't believe me.
God's power is strong.
Come and see, come and see!

It was such a strong knock on the outside door. Only a man with big strong arms, someone used to working with his hands, like a fisherman or a carpenter, would knock like that.

I'm only thirteen. I care for the two small children of my mistress, and fetch water, and make meals. I'm not paid a wage, because I'm a slave. I'm lucky my mistress is easy with me. She lets me take part in the gathering of Christians at the home of Mary, John Mark's mother, especially at the end of the day.

This particular night, I was sitting near the door. When I heard the knock, I ran to see who was there. I didn't open the outside door, though. It was dark, and the knock was so strong, it was frightening.

I'm only thirteen, you know.

"Who's there?" I called out.

A deep voice answered. I recognized it at once. It belonged to Peter, one of our Christian leaders. But how could that be? We all knew that King Herod Agrippa had put him in prison.

"Who's there?" I called again.

It **was** Peter's voice! That meant Peter was out of prison! I would know his voice anywhere. He used to tell us stories about Jesus every time we met. It was **Peter's** voice. No doubt about it.

I was so excited, I didn't think to open the door. I rushed back to the prayer meeting.

"Peter is standing at the outside door," I exploded with joy. "God has set him free." I flung my arms up in rejoicing. "Come and see!"

"You're out of your mind," jibed one man.

"It can't be him," sneered another. "He's in Herod's dungeons."

"You're mad, child," hissed one of the women.

I lowered my arms. They didn't believe me. I'm only thirteen, and a girl.

"But it's true," I persisted. "I would know his voice anywhere." I was practically squealing with excitement. I was absolutely sure it was Peter. I'd heard his voice outside the door, and they hadn't. Why did they not believe me?

But of course, I'm only thirteen. And a girl. And a slave.

Someone said, "It must be his angel. What you heard was not Peter but his angel."

KNOCK, KNOCK, KNOCK!

They all heard the knock this time. So they knew that someone was there. And it couldn't be an angel, because angels don't knock – they just appear with you.

"Come and see! Come and see!" I was almost shouting with excitement.

They came to see. I opened the door. There stood Peter! Everyone began to talk. All at the same time.

"How did she know?"

"I thought she was mad."

"How did he escape Herod's prison?"

"I didn't believe her. She's only a girl, and just thirteen, you know."

Peter held up his hand, and quieted everyone. He told them it was due to God's power that he had been freed. He asked us to tell everyone. Then he left us, quickly and quietly, because he knew Herod would be searching for him.

But I **knew** it was his voice. I would have recognized him anywhere. Why wouldn't they believe me?

Women at the tomb

Matthew 28:1–10; Luke 24:1–35

These women amazed us

"Church history begins when a few women set out to pay their last respects to their dead friend Jesus. It begins when, contrary to all reason and hope, a few women identify themselves with a national traitor, and do what they consider to be right... namely, never abandoning him as dead. Church history begins when Jesus comes to them, greets them, lets them touch him just as he touched and restored them in their lives. Church history begins when the women are told to share with the men this experience, this life they now comprehend, this life their hands have touched....

"Officially, church history begins with the mission of the men apostles, and officially, no women were present on that occasion."

(From Elisabeth Moltmann-Wendel and Jurgen Moltmann, "Becoming Human in the New Community," in the *Community of Women and Men in the Church*, p. 29)

The most convincing evidence for the resurrection is the emergence of a community of believers in history, of which we today are one small part. Something of earth shaking and life-transforming importance took place on that first day of the week, at the first sign of dawn. Otherwise, the Christian community would have disintegrated, dissolved in despair and disappointment.

Additional convincing evidence is that the gospels tell many versions of the resurrection. If there were only one fixed story, it would make me wonder whether the event actually took place, or whether it had been "cooked up." Just as eye-witness accounts of a traffic accident vary in detail and emphasis, so the four gospel accounts of the resurrection tell different details, and have different emphases. For me, that adds to the credibility of the event.

Our story is about the women who had been part of Jesus' community since his days in Galilee – a group of women who followed Jesus right from the beginning (Mark 15:40 and Mark 1:16–20). Most people believe that the four fishermen of Galilee were the most important disciples: Peter, Andrew, James, and John. But a number of women came from the same context of small fishing villages at the north end of the Sea of Galilee. These women included Mary of Magdala, the mother of James and John, Salome, and many others. Although we hear nothing specifically about the daily work of these women, it can be safely assumed that they were just as engaged in the work of fishing and fish processing as were the four disciples. Their work is not mentioned in the biblical account because women in those days were defined, not in terms of their work, but by their relationships with men (e.g., mother of the sons of Zebedee), or by their presumed place of origin (Mary of Magdala). These women, who had been with Jesus from the beginning, were the first to experience the power of resurrection in a renewed community life (Matthew 27:55 ff., Mark 15:40–41, Luke 23–24:11).

The fact that their witness and experience was initially denied by the male disciples does not diminish their faithfulness. Later, after some checking out of the women's story by the male disciples (Luke 24:22–25), two persons on their way to Emmaus speak of "certain women who astounded us... and declared he was alive."

These women amazed us

What's the matter with those men
who don't believe a woman's words?
Don't they know we're equal with
all of them – except the nerds!

I was up before dawn. The sun was standing on tiptoe, waiting to burst into a new day. My mom had asked me to gather together her spices and ointments. The women always used them to prepare a body for burial.

On the way to the burial place, we were joined by several other friends of my mom's. "Who will roll away the stone?" one of them asked my mom. Jesus had been placed in a cave carved out of the rock, called a tomb. A huge stone had been rolled across the entrance. All the women murmured in low tones. I couldn't make out exactly what they were saying. But they were worried that they weren't strong enough to roll the stone away.

Suddenly, the earth began to shake under our feet. I fell down face first in the mud. It was scary. When I looked up, the stone sealing the tomb was sitting **beside** the tomb. Sitting on it was an angel of God. His robe was as white as the snow that sometimes falls around here. He was fat and jolly. He smiled at us.

"Don't be afraid," he said. "I know you are looking for Jesus. He is not here. He has risen, as he said. Go quickly and tell his male disciples. You will see him in Galilee."

In Galilee! That was our home. That was where we had first met Jesus. And he would meet us there again! I couldn't believe it.

My mom could. She grabbed me by the hand. I could tell she was as excited and as happy as I had ever seen her. We quickly left the tomb. We scrambled as fast as we could over the cracks and big rocks that the earthquake had thrown up.

Suddenly, on the path ahead, was a man. "Greetings," he said. My mom and the others knew him at once. It was Jesus. They all fell on their knees before him and clasped his feet. They were crying.

How could this be, I wondered. It was scary for me. I was afraid.

"Don't be afraid," he said, looking right at me. "Go and tell my brothers that they must leave for Galilee. They will see me there."

"I knew he would always be with us," exclaimed my mom, as we hurried on. "He promised us."

The room where the men disciples sat was quiet. All the men were sad. Then the women burst in on them.

"He has risen!"

"He greeted us!"

They didn't believe us.

"Of course it was him. What do you take me for? We touched him!"

"We're not mad! Believe us!"

"You're to meet him too. In Galilee."

And the men responded:

"Impossible. He's as dead as a doornail."

"It must have been a look alike. Or your imagination is working overtime."

"You're full of idle tales."

"It's all nonsense...."

Peter wanted to believe the women. So he took John, and they ran to the tomb. Amazing – they found everything exactly as my mom and other women had said. "I suppose they think they have to check out our story for themselves," complained one of the women.

"Just like a man," said another.

"Not one of them ever apologized for not believing us," grumbled a third.

In the end, the women and the men made their peace with each other. My mom said, "Now we have to live a different kind of life together. Now we learn to depend on each other, sharing sad and happy times. We must make sure the hungry and poor are treated justly. We must make sure no one feels left out – even the animals and the plants."

I was glad she said that. When I got home, I patted my favorite cedar tree, and told it what my mom had said.

This man amazed us

Adapted from a true story told by Rev. Jim Christie, Southminster United Church, Ottawa

My dad visited San Francisco last summer. He went to help celebrate the 50th anniversary of the founding of the United Nations. I'm not sure what the United Nations is, but my dad thinks it's pretty important. I think it has something to do with keeping peace in the world.

Anyway, he'd never been to San Francisco. He knew he would have to get on public transportation to reach the hall where the celebration was to happen. The trouble was, he didn't know how much money he was supposed to put into the wall machine. He needed to buy a ticket for the fast train that would take him to the celebration.

When he went into the train station, he noticed a young man curled up in the corner. He was sitting on the floor. He was dirty, and he hadn't combed his hair for days. For sure he wasn't going to any celebration.

The young man asked if my dad could give him any change. He was very hungry, and hadn't eaten since yesterday.

Usually, my dad tries to give some cash to people who need it. "I do it because I'm afraid of missing Jesus," he has often explained to me. Then he'd tell me the story Jesus told about feeding the hungry.

The way the story goes, a king separated the people from each other, the way a shepherd separates sheep from goats. He put the sheep on his right hand, the goats on his left. Then the king blessed those on his right hand. He said, "I was hungry, and you gave me food."

Those on the right were puzzled: "When did we see you hungry and give you food?" they asked.

"I tell you," said the king, "if you have fed one of the poorest and hungriest ones, it's like feeding me."

Here was a poor, hungry person. So my dad put his hand into his pocket and pulled out most of his change. He pressed it into the hand of the young man.

"Thank you," said the young man.

My dad read all the signs. They explained just how much his ticket would cost. It wasn't very clear to him, a stranger. But he finally figured it out. The ticket would cost him $2.00. But when he checked in his pockets, he discovered he had only $1.90 left. He had given away the rest to the young man in the corner.

He began to talk out loud to himself, blaming himself for not keeping enough money to buy a ticket to get to the celebration. He hit his forehead with his fist. He was mad at himself.

Suddenly, the young man in the corner got up. He came to my dad.

"Here," he said, grinning broadly. "I think this is what you need."

It was a dime. It was a dime that my Dad had given him, just a few minutes earlier.

"Thank **you**," said my Dad with a huge smile. He bought the ticket, and got onto his train.

Women crossing boundaries

Dinah

Genesis 34

Crossing dangerous boundaries

Traditionally, this story has been interpreted as the rape of Dinah, who was understood to be the "property" of her brothers. They were Israelites and sojourners in the land which was the "property" of the Shechemites. One of them, Shechem, carried out the rape. The ensuing trickery and vengeance of the Israelites on the Shechemites was supposedly occasioned by the rape.

However, debate rages as to whether the story can be that simplistically interpreted.

An alternate interpretation is that Dinah, daughter of Leah and Jacob, was a victim, not of rape, but of brothers who were overzealous about what they believed was good for them and their tribe. The brothers' "property" (that is, one of their women) has been breached by an outsider, who showed lack of respect for the proper way of establishing kinship relations. Efforts at negotiation and mediation fail. Simeon and Levi, knowing their precarious position in the land, are not about to make peace with the "enemy."

The story intends to explain the continuing hostility between two peoples (the Israelites and the Shechemites) on the pretext of defending a woman's honor. What is at stake, though, is not Dinah's loss of status but the loss of face of her brothers who control her sexuality. The vengeance wreaked by Dinah's brothers following her rape has little to do with her feelings of unworthiness and shame after the rape. It has much more to do with the brothers' feelings about having their property violated.

Was she raped? A Hebrew scholar, Lynn Bechtel, makes the case against it. She thinks it may have been an illicit sexual liaison between Dinah and Shechem with mutual consent (Genesis 34:3), considered shameful because Dinah and Shechem were not of the same tribal group. She has brought shame on the tribe by consorting with an uncircumcised outsider. She crossed the tribal boundary. Bechtel emphasizes how the attempted bonding between Dinah and Shechem is paralleled by Jacob's efforts to bond with the Canaanites in a different way (Genesis 34:5–12). Yet both attempts are thwarted by Simeon and Levi, who place their own individualistic concerns ahead of the well-being of the community.

Alice Ogden Bellis, in her book *Helpmates, Harlots, Heroes,* refers to a very interesting attempt to seek connections between the past and the present. She refers to the work of Ita Sheres, a native of Israel, who draws parallels between the story of Dinah and the Israeli-Palestinian conflict. Levi and Simeon are the fanatical Israelis who will use any excuse to annihilate the Palestinians. Dinah is like the Israeli doves, mostly women, who would like to talk with the Palestinians. Like Dinah, they are quickly silenced. Crossing tribal boundaries may be a difficult, even impossible, way to bridge animosities.

No matter how you interpret the story, one fact is clear – no one showed any concern for how Dinah may have felt. She never speaks. She is never vindicated. She is forgotten. Her identity as the daughter of Jacob and the sister of Levi and Simeon is always determined by her relationship to a male relative. She is central to the story, but also always on the border, reflecting women's actual economic and social roles in that traditional culture.

For further reading

Bellis, Alice Ogden. *Helpmates, Harlots, Heroes: Women's Stories in the Hebrew Bible.* Westminster/John Knox, Louisville, 1994, pp. 87 ff.

Newsom, Carol A. and Sharon H. Ringe, eds. *The Women's Bible Commentary.* Westminster/John Knox, Louisville, 1992, pp. 23 ff.

Crossing dangerous boundaries

Dinah wept and Dinah cried;
She brought her family shame.
Her bigger brothers killed and lied,
To win their deadly game.

Her weeping could be heard in all of the tents of her father Jacob's household, pitched near the Canaanite city of Shechem. Dinah's world had collapsed around her. She lay on her mat, her tousled hair buried in the pillows, her despair and agony complete.

She was the only girl in her family. There were no sisters her age to talk with, and her mother Leah seemed too old. So Dinah didn't even raise her head to answer her mother's pleading questions. She felt that her life was finished. She was 15.

Quietly Leah slipped out of the tent. She summoned Dinah's childhood nurse, Miriam.

"Go to Dinah," Leah said. "She is feeling too badly hurt. She can't or won't talk to me. But she has told you all her secrets since childhood. Maybe she will talk to you once again."

For a long time Dinah refused to lift her head. Her beautiful face was streaked with tears and puffed with crying. Miriam held Dinah's head in her lap and stroked her hair. She remembered all the good advice she had tried to give Dinah about being the only girl among so many brothers. As a consequence, Dinah had become very strong willed and a bit of a rebel.

Suddenly Dinah sat up and yelled, "Why did this happen to me?"

She threw a pillow at the wall of the tent.

"Shh! Calm down, Dinah."

"Don't shh me! Just tell me why this happened to me?"

"Because you wandered off alone into Shechem, Dinah. None of this would have happened if you had stayed here among your own people. There are young men here for you."

"Who is there for me here? Just my father's servants and my own relatives. Besides, I only went to visit the women in the strange land we've come to," protested Dinah defiantly.

"That may be so, Dinah. But in fact the stranger from Shechem is not for you. He is not one of us."

"What does that matter?" screamed Dinah. "He spoke tenderly to me. I could come to love him, even if he is not one of us."

She held her head in her hands and rocked back and forth on the mat.

"Dinah! Child! Think! He disgraced and shamed you," she said, stroking Dinah's hair.

"No, he didn't." She looked away from her nurse. "Well, at first... at first he forced me a bit, but he did it because he couldn't help himself. He told me he loved me at first sight and that's why he took me. I believed him. Always he spoke softly to me and held me close. He respected me. He wanted to marry me," she sobbed.

After a time she continued, "My own father and brothers made an agreement with Prince Shechem and his father and tribe and I was going to be his wife until my brothers Simeon and Levi did what they did. Spoiled everything. I want to die."

She again held her head in her hands and rocked back and forth on her mat.

"Shh, Dinah." Miriam tenderly stroked Dinah's hair again. "Don't forget he was from an enemy tribe. To be his wife would have been impossible for your brothers to accept."

"My brothers!" She threw another pillow at the tent. "They don't care what I think. They never asked me what I feel. I might as well be one of their camels. Just because they want to protect our tribe from strangers, they murder my beloved. They weren't satisfied to avenge what they call 'my honor' by killing my lover and his father, but every man in the whole city. Then they stole their herds, looted their tents, and took all the women and children for their own slaves. Don't talk to me about 'honor.' They did all those murderous deeds to save face themselves with their own tribe. It was **their** honor they were worried about. Not mine! I want to die...."

"There, there, Dinah," murmured Miriam as she stroked Dinah's hair and hugged her tightly.

"What chance do I have now to get married?" Dinah moaned. "If they'd just stayed out of it, I could have been the Princess of Shechem." She pushed Miriam away roughly. "I've been shamed. I feel like a piece of dirt. Leave me alone."

Suddenly she sprang to her feet and threw another pillow at the tent wall. A final pillow sailed after Miriam as she made a hasty exit.

Women in black

Spat on by her own people

Crossing boundaries is one of the hardest things we humans are called to do. This story is based on the contemporary women's peace movement in the Middle East, where women try to heal the breach in the Israeli-Palestinian conflict. It builds on the Dinah story, and has some parallels.

Spat on by her own people

I'm just a girl, and only seven
But I want peace.
All this fighting and killing
Must soon cease.

My name is Miriam. I am seven years old. I live in Jerusalem. I've lived there all my life. My family are all Jews. I love living in Israel, except for the fighting and the guns and the suicide bombers.

On Friday afternoon, I went downtown with my mom. She goes every Friday. We took a sign that I had made. In the biggest, boldest letters I could make, it said, "We want peace with Palestine."

We stood in the middle of one of the main streets. We blocked the traffic! Cars and trucks screeched to a stop when they saw us. But it wasn't just us. There was a big group of women and girls. We caused a lot of nuisance. Some men shook their fists at us. Maybe it was because they couldn't get through the traffic jam we caused.

A few months ago, my Mom joined a group called "women in black." So she wore a black dress. I was all in black too. So was everyone else. There was even a dog with a black coat. The "women in black" want to stop the fighting and war where we live, the war between Jews and others who are different from us must soon cease.

There were lots of posters. One said, "Stop the killings!" Another said, "Peace in our time!" One kid rode a bicycle with its wheels all decorated in black, to mourn those who have been killed in this war.

Men swore at us. A woman came up and spat right in our faces. Without saying a word, I wiped the blob of spit off my face. Because we're for peace, we don't fight back.

Two weeks ago, three of our friends had to jump out of the way of a car that skidded right into them, when they were waiting for a bus. My mom thinks it was deliberate. She says the driver wanted to injure our friends.

People spat at us because in Jerusalem there are those who hate the people who are not Jews, but who live in Israel. Mom says these people who are not Jews call themselves Palestinians. Some of their families have lived here a very long time, just like mine. So they want to stay here too.

They don't go to synagogue. Some of them go to the mosque, and some to church. The boys wear these cloths around their heads – they call them "kaffeyiahs." I think it started because they needed protection against the sun, but I don't really know.

Anyway, they don't talk to us. And we don't talk to them. If a Jew accidentally bumps into one of them on the sidewalk or the street, it usually starts a fist fight. If one of them hogs the sidewalk, our people snarl insults at them.

But my mom and I and the other women in black think that fighting and killing is the wrong way to settle differences. We want to talk with girls whom we have been told are our enemies. That's why the women in black are sometimes called "peace doves." It's not a popular thing to do. That is why, when we take our posters downtown, they sometimes spit on us and swear at us.

I love Israel, my country. I love it just as much as the people who spit and swear. But it means that I want people to live together in peace. I've known the Bible story of Dinah since I was a toddler. I remember how she wanted to make peace with Shechem, who was considered an enemy. He was not of her race. He was an outsider. He was one of them. She thought that making peace was the right thing to do. But her crazy brothers started a war against the relatives of Shechem. Hundreds of people on both sides were killed.

It's so senseless.

Not many of my friends have joined the women in black. It's hard to reach out to people who are different. Besides, no one pays much attention to the voices of girls.

But I'm going to keep on trying. I decorated my roller blades with peace doves. I'm going to start a kid's roller-blade parade for peace every Wednesday after school. Right in the heart of Jerusalem!

Wish me luck.

An island girl

Accepting a stranger

Biblically speaking, the fact that women depended upon men for their identity and worth stopped them from developing a true and living solidarity with each other. The biblical text is filled with stories of women who had to compete with one another because they depended upon the same man.

- Esther, for example, had to compete with other beautiful young maidens to appear to the King as the fairest in the land.
- There are complicated stories about women whose dignity and substance depended upon their ability to bear children. Sarah and Hagar, Leah and Rachel and their two maidservants, all had to enter the competition for greater fertility (Genesis 29, I Samuel 1:30). Hannah and Penninah (I Samuel 1:2) also competed with each other.
- Women are depicted often as fighting with each other. Paul urged Euodia and Syntyche to "agree together" (Philippians 4:2).

But there are also stories of solidarity between women. Think of the story of the women around Moses. Think of the Exodus as the story of the strength, resistance, and determination of women. For many, the Exodus is the story of Moses and Pharaoh. But we know it began with two midwives, Puah and Shiprah (Exodus 1) and continued with the stories of his sister Miriam, his mother, Pharaoh's daughter, his wife Zipporah. (See stories in *Miriam, Mary and Me* under the section "Women's Initiative" in the Exodus stories.) But even some of these women had to express their solidarity in an "undercover" way so as not to be discovered.

There are other examples of solidarity between women. Naomi and her daughter-in-law Ruth formed a community of support for survival. Elizabeth and

Mary spent three months visiting and dreaming about how their future sons (John the Baptist and Jesus) could support and complement each other rather than compete.

What follows is a contemporary story of the friendship and solidarity that can exist between girls (and women by implication). It tells of how one girl looked beyond the common prejudices of her community to offer another girl the gift of acceptance.

Accepting a stranger

Based on a story in the Pacific Islands Christian Curriculum, Suva, Fiji, 1965

"Stu-u-u-pid and cross-eyed,
That's what you are, I swear,
I think you better go and hide,
'Cause you have dirty underwear."

That's the chant of the kids who live on one of the high islands in the Pacific ocean. They look down on the kids of a low island several hundred miles away in more ways than one. They think the low islanders are strange looking, slow and dirty.

The low island kids hurl back:

"Sticks and stones may break my bones,
But names will never hurt me."

One day, when the ship which sailed between the islands stopped at the high island, there was a boy from the low island on board who had leprosy. He and his older sister, who was along to care for him, were on their way to a hospital on another island.

The high island kids jeered:

"Leper, leper, go away,
Come again some other day."

The ship stayed at the high island for two days. On the second day, the boy's sister took a bundle of washing to the village spring not far from the dock. Kara, a girl of the village, was sitting on her porch and saw the low island girl walk by. A short time later, she saw the girl walking back toward the ship still carrying her bundle of dirty clothes. She carried her head high and refused to look at anyone else traveling along the path.

Kara thought to herself, "I know what has happened. The girls washing at the spring have refused to make a place for her by the water because they don't like low island people. They're scared they might get leprosy from her, because her brother has it. They think it's like AIDS or cancer. They don't know medicine can control it. I bet they're scared and that's why they're so nasty.

"But I bet she doesn't like high island people very much either. Especially not now. Now she has to take all of her clothes back to the ship unwashed. And she'll be hurt inside."

Kara felt sorry for this strange girl. She knew the girl must be angry because of the chant she had heard the high island kids yell at her:

"Leper, leper, go away,
Come again some other day."

But maybe the girl was also discouraged and lonely because of what had just happened.

Kara got up from the porch and walked to meet the low island girl on the road. She did not know the other girl's language. Kara smiled and motioned to the girl to follow her around to the side of her house. The low island girl looked at Kara suspiciously, but she decided to follow.

When they came to the back of the house Kara pointed to a big barrel of rain water. She made motions as though she were washing clothes.

The low island girl looked at Kara doubtfully. Why would this high island girl want to help her, she wondered? She hadn't done anything to stop the kids chanting at her. She hadn't done anything about the girls at the spring who closed her out. Maybe it was a trick. Or a trap. Or maybe it was to make her look stupid. She wondered if the high island girl had any idea how much she hurt inside.

Kara made the washing motions again. Still the girl didn't

move. Finally, Kara squatted, opened the girl's bundle and put some of the clothing in the water. It was enough. The girl smiled, stepped forward, and began the work of washing with Kara.

The girl stayed all afternoon. They made lots of hand signs and Kara learned about the girl's sick brother and why they were traveling away from home for medical treatment. She learned that leprosy was not something to be afraid of anymore.

Before the girl returned to the ship, Kara gave her some food. It seemed they were no longer strangers. That evening the ship sailed on its way.

Several months later the ship returned. Aboard it was a gift for Kara: a whale boat from the girl on the low island – something highly prized by high island fisherfolk. Kara had made a friend.

Naaman's slaves

2 Samuel 5

The little girl who could

This story is about a nameless Israelite girl who was slave to the equally nameless wife of Naaman. Naaman was a successful Syrian general. But he had leprosy. The slave maid, who had been captured in one of Naaman's battles, told her mistress about a Samaritan prophet, Elisha, who could cure Naaman.

The biblical story then jumps to Naaman persuading the Syrian king to send a letter to the Israelite king on Naaman's behalf, requesting a cure. The king could not, of course, cure Naaman. However Elisha the prophet heard about it and asked that Naaman be sent to him. You may remember the outcome of this story, from having heard it before; or you can read the rest of the story in 2 Kings 5.

I've told the story here in two parts. Part one is told by the Israelite slave girl, whom I have called Fridelle. But because she couldn't possibly be present for the second part of the story, it's told by her friend Joel, Naaman's slave, also a captured Israelite.

Traditional interpretation makes Elisha the central figure of the story. The power of Elisha's God Yahweh, even over kings and generals, is the main emphasis. Secondarily, the story is about Naaman, the mighty commander whom the prophet heals.

However, Naaman's nameless wife and a nameless Israelite slave girl made the story happen. The fact that they were not named is evidence of their inferior role in a patriarchal culture. The little girl knew her own religious tradition, and remembered Elisha and Israel. The two women compassionately did what needed to be done, yet are assigned minor roles in the story. They are completely dropped from the main action and credits as the story unfolds.

Yet their pivotal role needs to be acknowledged. Often people behind the scenes effect change, but get no credit. Many women and most children fall into this category.

For further reading

Laffey, Alice. "Thanks to a Nameless Maid: Naaman's Cure of Leprosy," in *An Introduction to the Old Testament: a Feminist Perspective*. Fortress Press, Philadelphia, 1988, pp. 136 ff.

The little girl who could

I think I can, I think I can,
Assist Naaman the Syrian,
Make him clean, make him good;
I knew I could, I knew I could.

I am eight years old. My name is Fridelle. I am a slave girl. My mistress, whom I love very much, never calls me Fridelle. When she wants me to bring her fruits or prepare her bath or deliver a message for her, she calls me "Hebrew maid" or "Little one."

I've been a slave to her ever since my friend Joel and I were captured by her soldiers in a raid the Syrians made against my people, the Israelites. Joel is 12. I still cry a lot in the night. I have not seen my father and mother since that battle when I was taken as slave. I know my father and mother loved me and called me Fridelle. My mistress, even though she loves me, never calls me by my name. But Joel does.

Joel is a servant to our master Naaman. Naaman is a very important person in Syria. He lives near a river. He has received medals and lots of money from the king because of his bravery and courage in battle. My mistress is so proud of him. But one thing makes her sad.

"It's a terrible thing," Joel whispered to me one night. "My master Naaman has the dread disease of leprosy. His skin has turned white and ugly."

"I think I can help him," I whispered.

"Really?" sneered Joel. "How can you help him? You're only a slave girl. Besides, Naaman is a very important person."

"I wish my master would go to see the prophet of our people in the land of Israel. He could cure him of his leprosy," I said firmly.

"Who is he?" Joel asked curtly. And then, doubtfully, "How do you know he can cure leprosy?"

"His name is Elisha. I remember two friends of my father who used to visit us. They were very important persons, just like Naaman. One of them had been cured of leprosy by Elisha. He is well-known in Israel as a prophet of God who can help. I think he can."

"Nobody would believe you," sneered Joel. "You're only eight years old."

I was silent.

But to myself I thought I would try to speak to my mistress about the master. I do care a lot about my Syrian mistress, even though she never calls me by my own name, and I know she loves me. I wondered if she would listen to me. I wondered if I had the nerve to tell her about Elisha.

To myself I said, "I think I can, I think I can."

Aloud, I said to Joel, "I'll try to speak to my mistress. I think I can."

One day I could.

My mistress spoke with her husband Naaman about what I could. Naaman spoke with the king about my mistress speaking with him about what I could.

The king spoke to Naaman about what my mistress had spoken to him about what I could. "Go to Israel," he said, "and I will send a letter to the king there, asking that he may cure you of leprosy."

And Joel got to go with Naaman.

I'm so glad I spoke to my mistress.

I knew I could. I **knew** I could.

The little boy who knew she could

(Joel's story to the nameless maid.)

I thought you might, then knew you could,
Help my master (touch wood!)
Into the river seven times,
He was cured, and that's my rhyme.

Naaman took me with him to Israel. Naaman is a very important person. We took lots of silver and gold and fancy clothes as presents. We delivered the letter to the King of Israel. When the king read the letter, he was so mad he crumpled the letter in his fist, shook his fists at his courtiers, tore his beautiful cloak from top to bottom, and yelled at the top of his voice:

"Who does this man think I am? Am I God? I'm only a king! I can't cure a man of leprosy. He's just trying to pick a fight with me and make me look foolish."

He stamped his feet, threw his crown at the nearest slave, and glared at us, so we hastily backed out of the throne room. It seemed so hopeless.

Then I remembered you, Fridelle, saying to me:

"I think I can, I think I can
Assist Naaman the Syrian."

The next thing we knew, your famous prophet Elisha heard about us. He sent word to the king to have my master, Naaman, come to him.

My master Naaman's strong horses galloped up to Elisha's house, drawing the silk-lined chariots behind them. But nobody came out to greet us. Elisha was nowhere in sight.

"I thought he invited us here," my master mumbled.

The mumble turned into a rumble. "So where is he?"

And the rumble turned into a bellow. "Is that him?"

I looked and saw a young man coming toward us. He bowed deeply before my master.

"I am only a humble messenger for Elisha," said the young man. "His message to you is this: 'Go and wash in the Jordan River seven times. Then you will be cured.'"

"Nonsense!" muttered my master. "Elisha has insulted me.

"I thought he would come out of his house," he cried.

"I thought he would stand before me," he screeched.

"I thought he would pray over me," he yelled.

"I thought he would wave his hand over my head," he shrieked.

"I thought he would order the leprosy to leave my body," he howled.

"I thought he would do something wonderful," he roared.

"I am a very important person," he screamed.

Suddenly there was dead silence. Then in a scary whisper, he started in again. "Instead he wants me to wash seven times in the Jordan River."

His voice got louder and louder. "Are not the rivers of my own country, Syria, better than all the rivers of Israel?"

He got madder and madder. "Does he think I'm a fool?" he raged. "Doesn't he know I'm a very important person?" he stormed.

His anger was as strong as a hurricane. In his fury he threw his spear as hard as he could at Elisha's house. He was ready to order us to turn the chariots around and race back to Syria.

My tongue was so dry with fear that it stuck to the top of my mouth. But I remembered that you, Fridelle, had spoken up when nobody else had. I repeated to myself what you kept saying:

"I think I can, I think I can
Assist Naaman the Syrian."

So I spoke. Kneeling before my master, I said, "Mighty commander, we all know you are a very important person. You who are like a father to us, wait a little. If Elisha had ordered you to do some hard thing, would you not have done it? Why not then do the easy thing he has said?"

My master fell silent for some time. Then abruptly he turned the chariots toward the Jordan River. He dipped himself in the water seven times. His skin became as soft as that of a small child.

Fridelle knew all along. It couldn't have happened without her. She kept saying, "I think I can, I think I can." I didn't have her faith in God. But I had faith in Fridelle. I knew she could. I **knew** she could.

Strong Women

Rizpah

2 Samuel 3:7 and 21:1–14

Vigil for her dead sons

Rizpah was a widow, a mother whose two sons were murdered, and a former concubine of Saul – all at the same time. She was, therefore, triply insignificant. Yet her spirituality of resistance to the culture of death enabled her to re-imagine and demonstrate a culture of life. It was so strong that even King David could not ignore it.

David believed that a three-year famine was continuing because of the guilt of Saul in murdering the Gibeonites. David acted to do two things at once: to placate the grievance of the Gibeonites, and at the same time to consolidate his own position and remove any threat to him or his heirs. During hard, male, elitist negotiations, the Gibeonites insisted that gold and silver were not enough compensation for Saul's abuse. They asked that seven of Saul's descendants be handed over to be executed. In those days, one of the methods of public execution was to impale the body – that is, to thrust a sharp stake through the body, and leave it hanging there to rot. That suited David's purposes just fine. So the seven were impaled on the mountain top in the first days of the harvest – ironically, during the time when the community collected the life-giving fruits of its hard work.

Rizpah's two sons were among the seven executed.

Rizpah kept vigil night and day over the bodies of her two sons as well as the others, exchanging the queenly robes of a concubine for sackcloth. For about five months, night and day, she protected their bodies from being ravaged by wild animals or vultures.

By her persistence in keeping their memory alive, she finally shamed David into gathering up the bones of those who had been shamed and giving them a proper reverent burial. David also gathered up the bones of Saul and Jonathan, and buried them in the grave of Saul's father Kish.

Up to that point David hadn't bothered to pay honor to his former enemy Saul. Indeed, Saul's remains, nailed to a wall at the site of his final defeat by the Philistines, had been left to rot. His faithful followers in the city of Jabesh retrieved the remains and buried them under a tamarisk tree (1 Samuel 31:8–31) – hardly a burial fit for a King!

David's reconciling action in ordering a proper internment for Saul's bones in his father's grave was welcomed as an act of justice and reconciliation. After this was done, "the Lord accepted prayers offered for the country" (2 Samuel 21:14). His act coincided with the return of the rains – which the biblical storytellers interpret as the interconnection of human life honored and nature renewed.

Why did Rizpah do it, since the seven men were already dead by the time she initiated her vigil? For the Hebrew people, life exists only in relation with other people. The possibility of being cut off from one's people is tantamount to death. By remembering the dead person, that person is linked with the community. Mutilation of the body and forgetting are the worst humiliations a person can suffer. Loss of memory of a person is accompanied by loss of identity of the deceased.

Rizpah took control where she could. In protecting her sons from further violation, and from the loss of remembrance of them, she demonstrated what it means to be human even in a terrible time. Her defiant act was a profoundly spiritual resistance against the oblivion that results from forgetfulness of persons. It was also a political act of resistance against male power and the culture of death.

Today, all over the world, many mothers have suffered the "disappearance" of their sons and daughters. They know no burial place. Rituals are therefore very important in preserving the memory of lost ones. In Latin America's prayers, often the name of the "desaparecidos" is called out as "present" in the believing community's rituals. It is a way of choosing life over death.

Even here in Canada, many of the Chinese workers who built Canada's railway through the Fraser Canyon in British Columbia died on the job. Buried as paupers (which they undoubtedly were), often in unmarked graves, their relatives thought it essential to recover and re-bury their bones in China. The recently published novel, *Disappearing Moon Café* by Sky Lee reflects this need. The novel makes the point that they are Canada's "disappeared" – life goes on as though they had never been.

For further reading

Bellis, Alice Ogden. *Helpmates, Harlots, Heroes: Women's Stories in the Hebrew Bible*. Westminster/John Knox, Louisville, KY, 1994, p. 144.

Cassidy, Sheila. *Audacity to Believe*. Collins, Fount Paperbacks, 1978.

Inter-Church Committee for Human Rights in Latin America (ICCHRLA) publications, 129 St. Clair Ave. West, Toronto, Ontario, M4V IN5

Lee, Sky. *Disappearing Moon Café*. Douglas and McIntyre, Vancouver/Toronto, 1990.

Vigil for her dead sons

I wouldn't give up
I would not forget,
My sons are not sticks
They're persons – you bet!

I couldn't believe it at first. David handed over to his enemies the two sons I had by Saul along with five of Saul's grandsons.

I can understand why he did it. Getting rid of Saul's offspring was the best way of making sure he got the throne. Those seven boys had no choice. They were caught in a political game.

It was just at the beginning of the barley harvest. There had been no rain for months. The fields were parched. There hadn't been much food for three years.

I learned that our enemies, the Gibeonites, were going to take my boys to the mountain top. Then they'd torture them by thrusting a sharp stake through their living bodies, and leaving them there to scorch in the desert sun until they died of their injuries. And they'd stay there until they rotted.

O God, help!

When I first heard, I fell to the ground. I pulled my cloak tightly around me, and moaned and cried for two days. I took nothing to eat. I ached in every part of my body. My face was swollen with weeping. I had nightmares about that dark mountain, and of the bodies pierced through by sharp stakes. I was always awakened by noises in the night. I thought I heard bloodcurdling screams, begging for mercy; I could feel the stakes as if they were ripping through my own body.

O God, help!

For a while I was all alone in my crying and grief. But then friends came to sit with me and mourn. We sat in a circle facing each other. Our bodies rocked back and forth in our grief, wailing in our unspeakable agony. We comforted and hugged each other.

They brought bread and water and grapes. The water jug and

the food were passed around our circle. I couldn't keep anything on my stomach, but it was good to have my circle of friends with me. Every day I got good hugs.

Finally, our circle of friends even talked a little about my fine two sons. Everybody had known them, so they all had a special story to tell. How Armoni had hated lamb when he was a small boy, and how he used to pile his serving of lamb onto his brother's plate when his brother wasn't looking. How Mephibosheth had spilled all our dinner one night when he was small, but he told me with a straight face that the wind did it! How strong they had been, just on the verge of manhood! And Saul's grandsons – delightful boys who loved tricks and fun.

Our circle drew in more tightly when we slowly realized that David didn't plan on burying the bodies. He was just going to leave them to the vultures and wild animals to feed on. Surely he wouldn't be so cruel! It couldn't be. But it was!

Our circle of sorrow turned to one of anger. It was terrifying enough to have them murdered. It was worse to dishonor their bodies by not burying them. They were to be forgotten in our tribe – never mentioned ever again. That's what I couldn't believe when I first heard it. Nothing like that had ever taken place in Israel before.

On the third day my circle of friends helped me put aside my rich queenly robes which I had worn when I lived with Saul. I asked my maidservant for sackcloth. In between my tears I put it on. I let my hair down. Then I stumbled out to the mountain where the bodies of the men still hung on those terrible stakes. There was a foul smell of rotting flesh. The fierce sun had shriveled and blackened the bodies. They looked like scarecrows and smelled like rotten eggs. I was sick at my stomach. My legs were trembling so much that I had to sit down. Spasms shook my body.

When I saw the vultures picking the flesh off a leg I grabbed a big stick and scared them off. That night, my friends came to be with me. They made a circle around our flickering campfire. Each of them brought their own blankets. I made myself a bed out of more sackcloth, and sat on the rocks near the fire.

I didn't get much sleep. We lit torches from the campfire, and used the bright light to frighten off the lions and animals that came close, hoping to feast on my sons. I was scared and tired. I was thirsty. At first I couldn't be bothered even to wash my face or comb my hair.

For all the days of the next five months, my women friends came with food and water and prayers for me. The women took turns sitting with me. They took turns washing my hair and perfuming it with frankincense to ward off the ugly smells in the place. They brushed and braided my hair. They got me to wash myself with water they had brought, and they tempted me with luscious grapes, pomegranates, oranges and other good food. I began to feel better. I could even keep some food in my stomach.

We held tightly to each other's hands as we vowed to resist David's indifference to the preciousness of human lives. These murdered men were humans. Whatever David thought they had done, they deserved to be honored as humans.

Day after day it went on. Night after night. Dry as dust. No rain. The harvest had been taken in. Even the fields were brown or yellow and seemed dead. I kept praying for my country, but God didn't answer. Why was there only silence?

I thought of my two sons before they were born. How I used to spin dreams of what they would do with their lives! How wondrous it was when they came out of me as live human beings – breathing, howling, with their perfect little hands and feet. What a miracle! And now, all that was not only wasted, but was to be forgotten.

No, I decided. I will not forget them. So did my friends. They stayed on and on with me until finally, it started to rain. The heavens opened and God's sweet merciful rain fell upon their bones. The fields looked greener. The little hills clapped their hands. God smiled on me.

One bright morning we saw some of David's servants arrive at the mountain. They looked around, held their noses, and then carefully edged over to where the remains of the bodies lay. They paid no attention to us. I scrambled over the rocks to them, and asked them what they thought they were doing.

"Orders," they said. "David says we're to take the bones and bury them honorably."

I could hardly believe it. I clambered over the rocks to tell my circle of friends that we had won! My murdered sons would now always be remembered. As we looked over that brooding mountain, we saw the servants gather up the bones and shovel them into a cart which they took with them. Our circle of friends had won over mighty King David.

God smiled again, and listened to the prayers we offered for our country. The mountains shouted their gladness, and the little lambs jumped for joy.

The mothers of May Square

This story is based on the history and true experiences of women in Argentina (1976–1985).

"I've never before seen trees dancing with large yellow flowers," I announced to my mother, as we walked arm in arm down a very wide street in Buenos Aires, Argentina. It was very warm. We were visiting that country for the first time.

There was something white on the sidewalk so I stooped and picked it up. It was a white cloth triangle big enough to wear on my head to keep the wind chill off, and it was decorated with blue embroidered lettering in Spanish.

"What on earth can it be, Mom?" I asked.

"Let's take it to a storekeeper over there and at least find out what it says," she responded.

The storekeeper couldn't speak much English, and we hardly spoke Spanish at all. But we did get the message that the blue embroidery was a name – "Paula" – and a date, "May 21, 1982."

"It might be important," I said to mother. "Let's take it to the police station. Probably someone is wanting it back."

We didn't get much of a welcome by the police. The constable at the desk glowered at us, refused to touch the head scarf, rudely snarled at us, and said something nasty about the "Madres de Plaza Mayo." My mom figured out that it had to do with mothers ("madres") and "Plaza" might be a central plaza called "Mayo."

We couldn't figure out why the policeman was so hostile to us. So we kept the scarf and went on our tourist way.

Presently we came to a spacious open place sporting yellow blossoming flowers on trees, and enormous pink buildings. We had arrived at the Parliament Buildings. There, incredibly, was a "Plaza Mayo" sign. Our English map had it marked as May Square! You could have knocked me down with a toothpick. The huge open space in front of their parliament was like our space for the Eternal Flame in Ottawa near our Houses of Parliament.

"Mom," I said. "Look at those women parading around in a circle. They're all wearing white head scarves with some Spanish writing embroidered on the top, just like the one we found. I wonder what it's all about?"

"Let's go and find out," Mom responded. "Maybe the owner of the lost scarf is here."

People were walking in an enormous circle that filled the whole plaza. They had linked arms – women with women, women with men. There were more women than men. As we got closer I could see that all the people walking had draped around their necks a cord holding something like a name tag. Each tag was plastic covered. Each one had a picture of a young person, a date, and a name. Some of the walkers were wearing three or four pictures. But the strangest thing was the complete and utter silence. No one spoke. No one laughed. No one cried.

"What's going on?" I whispered to my mom.

"Let's ask," she replied. She had made eye contact with a middle-aged stocky woman, one of the few who wasn't wearing a head scarf herself. She only had the pictures of two children around her neck. The woman came over to us when she saw my mother waving the white head scarf that we'd found.

She took one look at the scarf and then burst into tears! She traced each letter lovingly and pointed to each word on the scarf for our benefit. Then she pointed to herself. She was the owner of the scarf! She was Paula's mother!

She hugged us both, and summoned another woman to talk to us.

The other woman, Juanita, spoke English well. She explained to us what was going on.

"This is Maria-Therese," Juanita said. "She says it's almost like getting her daughter back again. For two years, ever since her daughter disappeared in 1982, she has walked in this plaza every Thursday. When she lost her head scarf last week, she thought that was it. Now she has it back, it gives her new hope."

Paula's mother, Maria-Therese, nodded vigorously.

"This silent vigil takes place every Thursday afternoon from two to four in the afternoon," Juanita explained. "A war is going on in our country between the rich government people and the poor. Soldiers are paid by the government to make sure no young person who protests against the rich goes unpunished. Any young person who helps the poor just 'disappears' from his or her home some night, never to be seen again."

I didn't believe what I was hearing. "How is that possible?" I asked.

"Usually it's a knock in the night. Soldiers come in and kidnap the young girl from her bed. Or it can happen in broad daylight. A car on the street pulled up beside my son Pablo. Soldiers hustled him into the car and drove off. I have never seen him since." Her voice broke for a second. "He and ten high school friends had agitated for cheaper bus tickets. This is his picture that I wear." She pointed to the picture of a boy hanging around her neck.

"But why don't you go to the police and ask where they are?" my mother asked.

"It does no good. The police just say, 'Your daughter isn't here.' 'We have no record of your son.' 'We know nothing about them.'"

We were struck dumb with her explanation. The silent march continued, a mute call for justice.

"You would be welcome to join us," Juanita urged us. "People from France, from Germany, from Korea, from Canada, from England, and from many other countries join in the march when they can."

"Do you ever expect to hear news of your son?" we asked Juanita, as we marched along, linking arms with the other women. "Does Maria-Therese ever expect to see Paula again?"

"No, never." She shook her head sadly. "I know in my heart that they have not only made them disappear, but that they will never tell us what happened to them. They are probably dead. But we keep their memory alive, hoping that some other young person will do the work with the poor that they would have done, if they had not been made to 'disappear'."

At four o'clock we kissed each other good-bye. Maria-Therese's farewell brought tears to our eyes.

"I believe in God above all else," she said as Juanita translated for us." Thank you for giving me my daughter back. I will never forget you."

Choosing life – a litany

This litany was used at the seventh Assembly of the World Council of Churches, Canberra, Australia, January 1991. It was authored by Chung Hyun-Kyung, a South Korean feminist theologian. It invites all to remember the oppressed of all the world by listening to the cries of creation and the cries of the Spirit within it. You might use it in conjunction with Rizpah's story. Adapt it as necessary.

Come, the Spirit of Hagar, Egyptian black slave woman, exploited and abandoned by Abraham and Sarah, the ancestors of our faith.

Come, the spirit of Uriah, loyal soldier, sent and killed in the battlefield by the great King David out of greed for his wife Bathsheba.

Come, the spirit of Jephthah's daughter, the victim of her father's faith, burnt to death for her father's promise to God if he were to win the war.

Come, the spirit of male babies killed by soldiers of King Herod upon Jesus' birth.

Come, the spirit of Joan of Arc and of many other women burnt at the "witch trials" throughout the medieval era.

Come, the spirit of the people who died during the Crusades.

Come, the spirit of indigenous people of the earth, victims of genocide during the time of colonialism and the period of great Christian mission to the pagan world.

Come, the spirit of Jewish people murdered in the gas chambers during the Holocaust.

Come, the spirit of people killed in Hiroshima and Nagasaki by atomic bombs.

Come, the spirit of Korean women in the Japanese "prostitution army" during World War II, used and torn by violence-hungry soldiers.

Come, the spirit of Vietnamese people killed by napalm, Agent Orange, or hunger on the drifting boats.

Come, the spirit of Mahatma Gandhi, Steve Biko, Martin Luther King Jr., Malcolm X, Victor Jara, Oscar Romero, and many unnamed women freedom fighters who died in the struggle for liberation of their people.

Come, the spirit of people killed in Bhopal and Chernobyl, and the spirit of jelly babies from the Pacific nuclear test zone.

Come, the spirit of students smashed by tanks at Kwangju, Tienanmen Square, and Lithuania.

Come, the spirit of the Amazon rain forest now being murdered daily.

Come, the spirit of Earth, Air, and Water, raped, tortured and exploited by human greed for money.

Come, the spirit of soldiers, civilians, and sea creatures who died in the bloody Gulf War.

Come, the spirit of women raped in Bosnia, of Tutsis and Hutus macheted to death by each other.

Come, the spirit of the Liberator, our Brother Jesus, tortured and killed on the cross.

In spite of the soldiers

My name is Esperanza. I am a 19-year-old girl. I am Mayan. When I was a child I lived in Guatemala. At about four o'clock one afternoon, the soldiers came to my village. The date was March 13, 1982, and the place, Rio Negro in my country. I was six years old then.

The soldiers wanted to drive us off the small plots of land where our families had lived for many years. Our parents and other fathers and mothers would not go. So the soldiers shot them. All I could hear were screams and moaning and bullet shots. I screamed too, but couldn't find my mother because everyone was running around, trying to hide.

Then they started to shoot children. I was huddled by the side of a pit where they were dumping the bodies of young children they had murdered. One of the soldiers spied me behind a rock. He said he would spare my life and take me to live with him. I found my baby brother, and waited with him. They grouped 18 of us children together, to take us to live with them in a town called Xococ.

By this time they had dumped earth in on top of the murdered children in the pit. They wanted to erase all traces of their crime. The soldier told me we had far to walk that night and that I wouldn't be able to carry my baby brother that far. I said I could. He said no. He grabbed my baby brother away from me, although I struggled and hit him and bit him. He tied a rope around the neck of my brother and was carrying him this way, choking him. Then he smashed my brother against the rocks, killing him, and threw him in the pit.

I was standing only ten meters away when this happened. Shocked and numb, I felt like jumping into the pit with him, but I was determined to live.

Around five o'clock we left Rio Negro. As we were walking, I heard some soldiers talking amongst themselves. One asked "How many did you kill?" One said 12, another said 15, and a third said 25.

Silvia, a mother whose family members were killed that day, escaped and fled to the mountains and lived in hiding for years.

She – and others of us who lived – did not forget.

Twelve years later, some of us, including Silvia and myself, came back to Rio Negro. It was 1994. We dug up the bones from the pit, carried them to a place where we buried them properly, offered prayers, and built a monument.

Within two weeks our monument was destroyed by soldiers.

A year later, a second monument was broken. "We are going to build a monument so big and strong that even a tank won't be able to destroy it," my people vowed. The killers destroyed the monuments because they didn't want the world to know about their crimes.

Finally, on March 12, 1995, a Monument of Truth, of steel and cement, was unveiled. It was three meters thick, four meters wide, and five meters high, and sunk two meters under the ground. We had built it secretly when church people from Canada were staying with us for a while. Their presence would have helped to protect us if the army had discovered us building the monument. The soldiers wouldn't want the world to know about their crimes.

Under the monument we buried the bones of 70 children who had been murdered at Rio Negro. A plaque reads:

CHILDREN WHO WERE SMASHED AGAINST THE ROCKS.

Until now, we have been afraid to speak openly about the crimes. The simple act of mourning our dead has led to more people being murdered. Meantime the guilty live and walk free. We pray for peace and justice to come to our land.

We do not forget the murdered ones. Nor does the God of Mercy.

Adapted from an article by Graham Russell, a human rights lawyer in Guatemala, published by the Campaign for Peace and Life in Guatemala, 1470 Irving Street, NW Washington, DC, 20010. For more information, you can get a video about the process of exhuming and reburying the children's bodies from EPICA, 1470 Irving Street, NW Washington, DC, 20010.

Herodias

Mark 6:12–31 and Matthew 14:1–13

He'll thank me, someday

My suspicions about the way the women in this story are portrayed were aroused by the reactions of a teen Sunday school class taught by my daughter. After reading the biblical story to them, she had the girls act it out. To her great surprise, the teens' dance was not seductive at all! My daughter advised me to re-read the story and try to find its real meaning. I discovered that John the Baptist was executed for reasons more complicated than those given us in the Gospels.

Our ideas about Herodias and Salome have been greatly colored by Richard Strauss's opera *Salome*. Salome's dance of the seven veils is pure imagination. Josephus the historian does not mention a banquet or even a dance, let alone one of seven veils. Moreover, it is extremely doubtful if Salome would have danced before such an audience since it was not becoming to her social status. The story bristles with historical difficulties.

What then could have been the motive for Herod's execution of John (which is historically accurate)? Could it have been a political motive, fueled by his desire to stay in power? The verses immediately preceding the story (Mark 6:12–13) speak of Jesus' increasingly popular work of casting out demons, and of anointing and healing the sick. Verse 14 says, "Herod knew of it; for Jesus' name had become known."

The Herod referred to here was Herod Antipas, one of the sons of Herod the Great, appointed Tetrarch of Galilee by Rome. Immediately Herod saw in Jesus another John the Baptist – criticizing his immoral court and evoking a mass movement which could easily turn into a threat to his power and popularity, and possibly into a first-class insurrection. That would place him in an embarrassing position with Rome, which expected its subject rulers to keep the peace at any price.

Herod had imprisoned John the Baptist in the fortress of Machaerus for attacking him publicly over his questionable morals. Herod had unlawfully married his brother Philip's wife Herodias. She had not only had an incestuous marriage with her uncle Philip, but then divorced Philip to marry her richer amd more powerful uncle Herod Antipas. Such a marriage was not legally valid from the Jewish point of view, and offended Jewish sensitivities. Both incest and divorce were regarded as shameful by every honest Jew. Although Herodias had lived long enough in Rome to be able to laugh at these scruples, she was highly unpopular in Galilee.

It is highly improbable that this single criticism would have provided sufficient grounds for executing so popular a person as John the Baptist. Could it have been a political motive, fueled by Herod's desire to stay in power? The historian Josephus, relating the death of John, implies this motive. He writes: "Herod feared that John's extensive influence over the people might lead to an uprising. He thought it much better to get John out of the way, in advance, before any insurrection might develop."

Herod wanted no truck or trade with the likes of John and Jesus. In his eyes, both were troublemakers, riding a wave of mass popularity. Their call to righteous living threatened him and his authority.

A feminist reading of this story raises a number of questions.

Salome is depicted (by common understanding) as one of the greatest adultresses of all time. But it was not her dance that decided Herod to murder John the Baptist. It may well have been the opportunity for him to murder the man who was a threat to his political power. But Salome doesn't deserve the bum rap the Gospels give her.

The biblical Herodias has no voice, and is smothered by implicit accusations, although non-biblical sources portray her as anything but a shrinking violet. It is her daughter Salome (so named by Josephus) who gets to address Herod. Why does Mark fasten the blame on Herodias? Does he depict her as a scheming woman because of her unethical liaison first with Philip and then with Herod? Or because of her attempt to influence politics? Because she outraged Jewish sensibilities by her marriages? Because she was linked with Roman overlords who ruled the Jews oppressively?

And why is Herodias not included in her own husband's birthday celebrations? Salome has to go outside the male banquet to consult with her mother. Herodias was without a doubt a "bad apple," but why is she presented as totally evil, while both men are credited with goodness?

John the Baptist is certainly a righteous man – even Herod recognized his moral goodness and, to his credit, kept John safe for some time. Yet Herod's evil side is not depicted. He offers Salome "whatever you ask me... even half my kingdom." The hypocrisy of this offer is never unmasked. Herod Antipas had been given the honororary title of "King" by his Roman overlords, but it was never in his power to give away half of "his" kingdom because he didn't have a kingdom to give away. Yet he is depicted as benevolent.

By my reading of the text, Herodias was a strong woman who had to struggle to be visible at all in a patriarchal context. She undoubtedly harbored a grudge against John for calling her to righteous living. But more than that, she feared he could be instrumental in overturning Herod's court, with a subsequent loss of political power for herself. Whether she alone deserves to be portrayed as the epitome of evil is another question.

What follows is an imaginative reconstruction of her story.

For further reading

Fiorenza, Elisabeth Schussler. *But SHE Said: Feminist Practices of Biblical Interpretation.* Beacon Press, Boston, 1992, pp. 48–50.

Graves, Robert. *Claudius the God.* Penguin Books, Toronto, 1934, pp. 2–23. Includes a geneological chart, clarifying the relationship of Herod the Great to his three sons (Philip, Archelaus, Antipas) as well as the situation of Herodias and Salome and the biblical references to these historical characters.

Kee, Howard Clark and Franklin W. Young. *Understanding the New Testament.* Prentice Hall, NJ, 1957, pp. 28–30, 82, 90–91.

He'll thank me, someday

I simply loved my Herod,
That's all I tried to do.
You may hear tales about me
But they're not all true.

I have loved my husband Herod for a long time. I tried to love Philip, but it never worked. He was such a wimp.

I have hated John the Baptist for a long time. My husband says this Jesus who has crowds of people following him is another John the Baptist! Their movement is becoming so strong, it threatens my husband's power. Why doesn't Herod **act**? Sometimes I think **he's** a wimp. After all, John spoke against Herod publicly, accusing him of being wicked. He said it was unlawful for Herod to have me. **Have** me indeed! Does he think I'm a piece of meat to be owned as if I'm property ? I'm much too strong for that nonsense. Does it not occur to him that **I** have **Herod**?

Herod says he is afraid of the people who think John is a prophet. If he moved against John, the people would rise up against us. Well, I know he wants to be rid of John. Maybe I can do what he's too scared to do. He'll thank me for it, someday.

I've thought a lot about it, and I think I have a good plan. It's all for the good of the kingdom too. And to keep Herod and myself in power. If we were to lose the throne there would be chaos.

Herod's birthday celebration is coming up. He'll entertain lots of guests. There will be wonderful food, too much drink, and dancing girls. My daughter Salome is a great dancer. There's no one better in this part of the world. I'll get her to dance at the court that night. And if custom takes its usual course, the king will promise to give her whatever she asks for. He's done that for the past few years. I'll coach her to ask for the head of John the Baptist on a platter! I would ask it myself, but I'm not allowed to attend the banquet. I'm a woman, not a dancing girl!

I think Salome will do that for me. Besides, she has no choice. I don't think I'm a wicked woman. I just know what's in the best interests of Herod and myself. This will put some fear into any other upstarts who want to overturn our rule. It's in the best interests of the people to have a stable ruler. A country needs a strong king whose authority is never questioned. I know how to help Herod do just that. I know he'll thank me for it, someday.

If this Jesus continues in the same way as John the Baptist, I may have to do the same for him. But it may not be necessary. Herod exaggerates about Jesus. This man Jesus is not as dangerous as John was. He's softer. I've heard he includes everybody in his circle and teaches love and mercy. That sentimental slop can't stand up against the might of Herod. The Jesus movement will fade away if we just let it run its course. I won't have to do anything.

You just wait and see! Herod will thank me for this, someday.

Salome

Mark 6:12–31 and Matthew 14:1–13

Old enough to look after myself

Not for young children

Herodias did, in a sense, sacrifice her daughter for her husband. Salome's story is, therefore, the story of a mother betraying her daughter (or at least using her daughter) for her own gain. In this case, the gain is Herodias' infatuation with Herod, the new man in her life, and the political power that goes with that man.

Do not tell this story to small children. It may disturb them to think that a mother's love for them can be usurped by a new man, for whatever reason.

But for teens and pre-teens, I think that this story does – unfortunately – reflect an all-too-common situation. Not every mother is a faithful mother. Sometimes women do try to please the men in their lives, and to protect their own social and political status, at the expense of their children. Sometimes, for the sake of some short-term gain or other, they do things that have long-term repercussions on their children. For that reason, I have not sanitized this story.

The story is, of course, also about the terrible dilemma that children may find themselves in when their parents break up. They are confused about their welcome at home, wherever "home" is.

In the end, Salome doesn't know what will happen to her. And history, in this case, is no help, because it makes no further mention of her.

The little verse at the top unfortunately reinforces the stereotypes about Salome's dance, based only on Strauss's erotic fantasies. Provided you and your children recognize that it has little basis in fact, it's probably harmless enough fun.

So here is Salome's story. I think it is best told to a pre-teen or teenager, but use your own judgment.

Old enough to look after myself

Salome was a dancer, she danced the itchy gitch,
She danced before King Herod, she barely wore a stitch!
King Herod cried, "Oh babe you're hot,
Oh babe you're in the money,"
But John the Baptist wailed, "By gosh, for me this isn't funny."

What am I supposed to do? Is there anywhere I can hide from my mother?

She's changed so much since she came to Herod's court. She wants me to do the same to Jesus as I had to do for John the Baptist. She's scared stiff of both of them. Jesus is so famous and he is my hero. I know Herod is afraid he'll lose his throne to Jesus. Of course, he thought the same thing about John the Baptist.

Mother thought John was a some kind of revolutionary threat to Herod's power and to hers. I think that's a stupid idea. But I'm only a young girl, so who listens to me?

That time with John the Baptist was awful. I was terrified. I didn't blame John for ticking Herod off about stealing my mother from my father Philip. John is the only person I've known who had the courage to tell it like it is. He let the whole world know how wicked and evil my stepfather Herod really is, and how he was the cause of my parents' breaking up their marriage. He was so brave. I loathe Herod. He's a creep.

It was Herod's birthday, I remember. No women were allowed at the banquet – thank goodness – because it turned into a drunken orgy. It was to be like all of Herod's parties, only bigger. We heard about them through court gossip. How I detest Herod!

But my mother Herodias knew that Herod wanted to be rid of John, because he was so popular with the people. It had to be done quietly. Any disturbance and the Romans would have got rid of Herod as a bumbling incompetent idiot, which he is, and taken over. My mother loved Herod's power so much she'd do anything to get in his good graces and keep her position. She's changed so much since she came to Herod's court.

It was at the women's banquet she made her proposal. It was that I be sent into the men's banquet to dance, since none of the women would be allowed. Everybody thought it a splendid idea. I'm old enough to look after myself so I did it. I'm a good dancer and my mother and the other women knew that. They also knew Herod would be pleased. I danced my best. But I was still bowled over when Herod promised with an oath to give me whatever I wanted. Weird old stepfather actually offering me whatever I wanted! There were tons of things I wanted to ask for, but mother had planned it all. She didn't realize that I'm old enough to look after myself and make my own decisions.

"Go back," she ordered me after I had rejoined the women's banquet to find out what they wanted me to ask for. "Ask to receive the head of John the Baptist on a platter. That will finish off John. And Herod will stop protecting him just because he is popular with the crowds. In the end, he'll thank me for what we're doing." I think my mother had invented this plot long before the women's banquet, long before she sent me in to dance before Herod.

I'm old enough to look after myself. I knew that what mother had in mind would also suit me very well. It was my chance to really-**really-REALLY** screw up Herod's life. I hated him for what he'd done to our family. He had no right. He was an evil evil man. I'm old enough to look after myself, and I had my own schemes to get back at Herod. I knew what would happen to him in the end. So I went along with mother's plot.

I returned to the men's banquet, screwed up my courage, and begged Herod for the head of John the Baptist on a platter. I had promised myself I wouldn't cry – not in front of Herod. Not until afterward. I'm old enough to look after myself, so I knelt down in front of him and implored him in my most winning voice for John's head. I could tell he was sorry I had asked for such a thing. But he didn't want to back down on his silly oath in front of all his male guests. He was a proud man. Besides, he really wanted to get rid of

John. So he sent the order to the prison and it was done.

I still get sick at my stomach every time I recall the platter being given to me with the bloody head of the prophet on it. It looked like a piece of meat for dinner. Blood dripped on the royal carpet. The eyes were bulging and sightless. I often cry myself to sleep and have nightmares about a headless body chasing me.

It was all my mother's idea. She knew that Herod didn't have the courage to do it. I'm old enough to look after myself, and it was a chance to do what I'd always wanted to do – ever since Herod scooped me into his household and ruined my relationship with my mother. It may not have been right, but I wanted to really mess up his life.

At least John's disciples came and took his body and buried it properly and reverently. Then they went and told Jesus.

I'm going to find a place to hide from my mother. Maybe I'll have to run away. I wonder if my real father, Philip, would take me back? When I had to "leave home" and come with mother to Herod's court, it was like a death sentence. I loved my father Philip dearly, and I would so like to live with him again. I think I remember the way to my father's house, but I don't know if he will welcome me. Would he feel that it's too great a risk to take me back when Herod rules the roost?

I have decided absolutely that I will never ever again go along with my mother just so she can "get in" with Herod and his powerful court – even if her plot also served my own wishes about that vile man. I'm old enough to look after myself now. It's just that I don't know where to go or what will happen to me!

Jephthah's daughter

Judges 11:1–40

Two months to never grow up

This story is not history. It is Hebrew "midrash" (commentary about a biblical story). It parallels two previous stories of potential human sacrifice.

The first one, of Abraham and Isaac (Genesis 22:1–18), is of God testing Abraham's obedience even to being willing to offer up Isaac as sacrifice. When it is obvious Abraham is prepared to proceed, an angel intervenes and provides a ram as a substitute sacrifice.

The second story is that of Saul and Jonathan (I Sam. 14:36). Saul, having received no assurance from God that he will have the victory over the Philistines, wonders where the guilt lies that makes God inscrutable. Jonathan admits to eating a little honey. Eating during battle is forbidden. Saul swears that Jonathan must be sacrificed, but the people won't allow it.

Although someone – an angel or the people – intervenes on behalf of the two male victims, no one intervenes on the girl's behalf in this story of Jephthah and his daughter. Is it because she is female? Or is it to lift up the absolute wrongness of human sacrifice?

Midrash gives the daughter a name, Sheila, and treats her as a great Talmudic scholar as she argues with formidable rabbinic scholars about child sacrifice. The emphasis is on a faithful daughter, in contrast to her faithless father. She is capable of saving herself, but the male-dominated world prevents it. She is raised to the status of a legendary heroine. Jephthah comes off as a fool. Perhaps there is more to this story than meets the eye.

The story was written during the chaotic and rough agrarian times of the Judges, around 1100 BCE, to strengthen support for a central power under a king by telling horror stories of disorder without a king.

Jephthah, the son of a prostitute who could not inherit his father's property, was driven away from home by his half-brothers. He was a first-rate fighter. He was made commander by the elders of Gilead to guarantee the defeat of their enemies, the Ammonites. In return for commanding the Gilead forces, he extracts a promise of a permanent political position as well as military leadership. This of course implies property. This negotiation is cemented at Mizpah, where, you may remember, Jacob and Laban sealed their distrust of each other with the vow which has become known as the Mizpah benediction: "The Lord watch between me and thee, while we are absent one from the other."

Jephthah bargained for victory by making a foolish vow (Judges 11). If God would give him a military victory, then he would sacrifice to God the first creature that came out of the door of his house upon his return. It turned out to be his daughter. Though overcome with grief, he manages to twist the story to blame her, the victim!

Traditionally the story has been interpreted as the daughter nobly embodying the ultimate patriarchal value, that of women being submissive to male authority, even unto death. In the *Women's Bible Commentary*, Danna Fewell notes, quoting Alexander Whyte: "As one turn-of-the-century interpreter wrote concerning the young women who yearly mourned Jephthah's daughter: 'They came back far better daughters than they went out. They came back softened and purified, and sobered at heart. They came back ready to die for their fathers, for their brothers, for their husbands, and for their God.'"

In this case, the expectation that daughters will submit to fathers, regardless of consequences, ends in a gross distortion of justice.

In spite of putting his foolish vow before his daughter's life, Jephthah died an exemplary Judge (Judges 12:7) according to the record, and "through faith did great things" (Hebrews 11:32). He has been immortalized in Handel's "Waft her Angels to the Skies" in the oratorio *Jephthah*.

His daughter asks only that she may spend two months in seclusion with her friends to laugh, to cry, to tell stories. The translation of verse 37 is "to bewail my virginity." Scholars Peggy Day and Norma Joseph both say that the term "virgin" does not carry the contemporary meaning of "untouched by a man." Rather, she and her friends are observing the ritual of the social recognition of puberty and transition to physical maturity. She is lamenting leaving childhood behind, and entering her menstrual cycle. When she goes to the hills she is not a "virgin" in our sense, but an "unmarried woman." This foundational legend of the female's rites of passage is claimed by her to institute a "women's space" or retreat for four days annually, which unfortunately has been lost in contemporary ritual. Phyllis Trible says that verse 40 should read, "She became a tradition."

Verse 39 says "She died a virgin." The word used here means "without issue." So Jephthah has robs not only her, but himself also, of progeny for the future.

Danna Fewell suggests that Jephthah's vow may well have been public, and Sheila knew of it. She intentionally challenges her father by appearing first upon his return, taking the place of someone he considered expendable. By so doing Fewell suggests, "she passes judgment on her father's willingness to bargain for glory with the life of another. Her action condemns his priorities, and those of Israel as well." Is it possible that she was not a victim, but a courageous young woman wanting to subvert the injustice of child sacrifice? That would certainly fit with the later midrash that elevated her to the rank of a great Talmudic scholar, arguing against human sacrifice.

If you have trouble with a pre-puberty girl taking such powerful initiatives as sacrificing her own life deliberately, consider her subsequent speech and actions. She takes control of the situation. She wins a reprieve of two months and retreats to the mountains with her friends. After that initiative she becomes a tradition in Israel. Not bad for a pre-puberty girl! And remember – this is midrash, not history.

It is difficult to read this text as a feminist. I think of at least three approaches to the story.

- First, I could see the daughter as a victim of male arrogance and stupidity (not an unknown story in today's world, either).
- Second, I would put the emphasis on women's solidarity and the way her friends rallied around her (again, not unknown today).
- Third, I could believe that she knew of the vow and courageously decided to allow the sacrifice, in the hope that such a horrifying tale would end human sacrifice forever.

It's the third option that I have tried in this story.

For further reading

Day, Peggy, ed. *Gender and Difference in Ancient Israel*. Augsburg/Fortress, Minneapolis, MN, 1989, pp. 58-74.

Bellis, Alice Ogden. *Helpmates, Harlots, Heroes: Women's Stories in the Hebrew Bible*. Westminster/John Knox Press, Louisville, KY, 1994, pp. 127-131.

Joseph, Norma. *On Hearing the Voice of Women in the Bible*. Lecture, "On Sacrificing Daughters" at a weekend retreat, March 1-3, 1988.

Fewell, Danna N. "Judges," in *The Women's Bible Commentary*, ed. Carol A. Newsom and Sharon H. Ringe. Westminster/John Knox Press, Louisville, KY, 1992, pp. 63-77.

Two months to never grow up

She was his only daughter,
As pure and fine as gold.
He chose to sacrifice her
When she was twelve years old.

I knew it would end this way. It's so horrible. It hurts so much. I'm scared. I can hardly breathe, it hurts so much. I'm terrified at the thought of losing my life because of a selfish vow my father made. I'm only 12.

Why did my father do it? He must have known he was bargaining for glory with the life of his dearest. Why did he value his victory as more precious than my life? I feel like nothing, worthless.

Of course he knew I had heard of his stupid vow at Mizpah – if God would give him victory over his enemies, he would sacrifice to God the first creature that came out of his house to meet him when he returned. Did he think it would be one of our servants? Or a house guard? Or a pet? Or a maidservant whom he wouldn't miss?

I bet in his wildest dreams he never imagined it would be me, his only child. Does he think his fleeting victory over his enemies is more important than any human life? What has he gained by being hailed as a big general, but sticking to his stupid vow that condemns his only daughter to death? That isn't what God wants – I'm sure of it. Why can't he break his vow for my sake? It's cruel that he puts his religious vow ahead of the sacredness of human life.

I go over and over in my own mind what he said when he saw me come to greet him. "Alas, my daughter, you have broken my heart, such trouble you have brought upon me. I have made a vow to God and I cannot go back on it." As if **I** had been the one to do something stupid. Then he wept. I'd never seen him weep before. It was agony for me to watch.

Anger mixes in my tears of grief. "Such trouble as you have brought on me" – I never brought **anything** on him. It isn't my fault. Dumb men! Why doesn't he admit he brought his ruined life on himself? But I don't have the nerve to say that to him.

I knew it would end like this. As soon as I heard the vow, I knew he should not have made it. It was not a noble idea. It was wrong to trade a military victory for a human life. But since God gave him and all of Israel victory on the battlefield, he had better do what he solemnly vowed. I hope it will shame all of Israel. I hope it will make all of them see human sacrifice for what it really is – not honor or obedience to God, but a shameful act. That's what I wanted to say to him as I hugged him and kissed his tears away. But I couldn't.

What horror! I could hardly speak. My tongue stuck to the top of my mouth, I was so scared. I shook like a leaf.

The only good thing is that my dearest girl friends are with me. For two months we will roam the hills, mourning the loss of our childhood and the loss of our chance to enter womanhood. After all, I'm 12 years old. It's such a beautiful thing young women do, and have done together for centuries. It usually is a time to wail over the end of childhood and the beginning of new possibilities and a dazzling future. Only I don't have a future. I never dreamed I would be joining in that ceremony with my friends out in the hills, facing what I must face. My friends have vowed that for four days in every year, the girls and women will roam the hills, remembering me. Forever. I hope so.

I hope they remember how wrong it is to bargain with God. And how wrong human sacrifice is.

And as for my father, I wonder if he has realized yet that there will be no descendants, no offspring, no heirs, to carry on his name. How sad that he brought it on himself.

Shekhinah

The question that wouldn't go away

The Christian characterization of Judaism as strict male monotheism disregards feminine and relational features of Jewish God language. God's diverse names in the Hebrew Scriptures have been interpreted by the rabbis as God's different aspects. While the Jewish tradition has maintained imageless monotheism, it has also created a rich pool of metaphors for the divine.

One such is *Shekhinah*, a post-New Testament Jewish idea. It implies God's female immanence, compassion, and co-suffering with people. *Shekhinah* was a rabbinical term. Underlying the use of the word "glory" is the belief in God's presence on earth. The Hebrew word for "dwell" is *sh-k-n* from which the post-Biblical word *shekhinah* is derived. The word carries with it the idea of God's presence among humankind. Those who live a devout life are worthy to see the face of *shekhinah*.

Associated with it also is the notion of "brightness," of light breaking through in splendor. *Shekhinah* is used today as a reverent reference to the feminine face of God.

Melchizedek, King of Salem and Priest of the Most High God (Genesis 14:18, and Psalm 110:4) refers to a priesthood more honorable even than Aaron's, a kingship greater than David's – the highest order of priesthood.

For further reading

Anderson, Sherry Ruth and Patricia Hopkins. "The Question That Won't Go Away" in *The Feminine Face of God: the Unfolding of the Sacred in Women*. Bantam, Doubleday Dell Publishing, 1991.

Richardson, Alan. "Melchizedek," in *A Theological Word Book of the Bible*. SCM Press, Bloomsbury St., London, 1950, p. 142.

The question that won't go away

This story was used by the Congregation Darchei Noam, Toronto, December 16, 1995, to celebrate the occasion of 11 women becoming *bat mitzvah* (coming of age spiritually). It is a shortened version of a dream that the author, Sherry Ruth Anderson, had in 1984. The full story is in her book *The Feminine Face of God.* It requires the reader to make a leap into fantasy and imagination. It's quite different from the other stories in this book, but I think it deserves to be included. I associate it somewhat with Jephthah's daughter, who certainly "came of age spiritually," if tragically.

"Shekhinah: the feminine face of God..."

The words sent shock waves rippling down my spine and goose flesh bristling on my bare arms because I realized at once that Shekhinah was not an uninvited guest at all. She had been announced to me with great ceremony in a powerful dream a full month earlier.

...I am dumbfounded by what I see. Rolled onto finely carved wooden poles is the most sacred object in Judaism, the Torah. I learned as a child that the Torah contains the five books of Moses written on parchment by an Orthodox scribe, and that if even one letter has been written incorrectly, the Torah cannot be used. I have never actually seen a Torah close up or held one, since these privileges were permitted only to men when I was growing up. But now I lift this Torah carefully out of its cabinet and cradle it to me tenderly as if it were a baby.

Then I notice something unusual. Instead of a mantle of velvet covering the scrolls, or a simple ribbon holding them closed, the Torah has been sealed shut by a dark round blot of red wax. I look at Melchizedek.

"This is a very special Torah," he says, "because what you need to know now is not written in any book. You already contain that knowledge. It is to be unfolded within you."

"What is in the Torah?" I ask.

My question seems to set in motion the next sequence of events. Without speaking, Melchizedek lifts the Torah and lightly places it inside my body, from my shoulders to my knees. I accept this gratefully, feeling my body as a sacred vessel.

At once a great commotion breaks out behind us. Spinning around, I see that the room is now filled with long bearded patriarchs wearing black coats and trousers. They're holding hands, laughing, singing and dancing jubilantly around the room. They pull me into their celebration. As I dance I seem to see Moses, King David and King Solomon, and Abraham, Isaac and Jacob. They too, are dressed in black coats and trousers, dancing with such heartfelt abandonment that I catch their joy and am filled with it. Ecstatically we whirl round and round the room, laughing.

Finally the dancing stops and I ask, "What is this all about?"

Melchizedek answers, "We are celebrating because you, a woman, have consented to accept full spiritual responsibility in your life. This is your initiation as one who will serve the planet."

As I wonder what this means, he continues, "And you are not the only one. Many, many women are now coming forward to lead the way."

"But who will be our teachers?" I protest.

"You will be the teachers for each other. You will come together in circles and speak your truth to each other. The time has come for women to accept their spiritual responsibility for the planet."

"Will you help us?" I ask the assembled patriarchs.

"We are your brothers," they answer, and with that the entire room is flooded with an energy of indescribable kindness. I am absolutely confident in this moment that they are our brothers. I feel their love without any question.

They say then, "We have initiated you and we give you our wholehearted blessings. But we no longer know the way. Our ways do not work anymore. You women must find a new way."

Job's wife

Job 2:1–9

Dealing with a dunderhead

Job's wife is a one-line character in the book bearing Job's name. She plays a small, but not insignificant, role in the story. She is crucial to the audacious questioning of the ways of God that her husband later takes up.

Most scholars read Job as a fictional story. The opening prologue depicts God as a torturing and unjust deity with little compassion for human misery. Job, by contrast, is a "righteous pious" man who has ten children (seven sons and three daughters), 7,000 sheep, 3,000 camels, 500 yoke of oxen, 500 donkeys, and many slaves. One day Job suffers a series of tragic events: he loses his property, his slaves, and his children. Later, he suffers a further, very personal, indignity: boils on his skin. Through all of this he does not curse God, but acts with too-good-to-be-true resignation and unlimited patience.

Through these trials, Job is held up as a paragon of virtue for his unquestioning obedience to what he sees as God's will. He is pious precisely because he does not believe in a God of mercy who forgives. God is simply to be submitted to – not to be questioned or challenged. Job's God is unyielding and unchangeable.

From Chapter 3 on, though, Job insists on his innocence, protests against injustice, and rages against God for visiting him with unspeakable suffering.

It is Job's wife (2:9) who changes Job from a patient to an impatient man. Seeing her husband sitting in the city dump, silently scraping the scabs off his boils, she bursts out, "Are you still unshaken in your integrity? Curse God and die."

Job was so honest (his "integrity") that he could not admit knowing of any sins that warranted his severe punishment. So why not pursue one's honesty, asks his wife? Even if it means cursing and challenging God.

Has Job's "perfect" devotion to a supposedly "perfect" God any reality? Not all suffering is the result of sin. Job knows this, but doesn't at first pursue that line with God. But his wife sees her husband's action as cowardice. What Job must do is challenge God. His put-down of his wife as "a wicked fool of a woman" is his last outburst before he capitulates and adopts her advice.

Chapter 3 opens with Job ready to curse his birth and the God who gave him birth. Job's wife endorses an impatient kind of faith, preferring protest against divine injustice to dogmatic, unthinking, patient faith. Prodded by her, Job realizes that God does not fit the fixed categories of "perfect" and "just." His faith stops being static and fixed, and becomes an ongoing quest.

The change, prompted by his wife, enables Job to change his approach to human relationships – with his friends, his wife, and eventually his children. He gives his daughters beautiful names and gives them property – both unusual acts in biblical history. He realizes that intense and questioning dialogue with God is as important as piety.

It is no accident, I'm convinced, that Job's wife is excluded from the closing happy narratives. Because she is seen as an "outsider" by the authors – a woman butting into what they see as her husband's business – her presence is viewed as threatening, and so she simply disappears from the text. Never mind, she has done her work. She avoids taking truths for granted.

For further reading

Pardes, Ilana. *Countertraditions in the Bible*. Harvard University Press, Cambridge, MS, 1992.

Pobee, John S., and Barbel Wartenberg-Potter. *New Eyes for Reading*. World Council of Churches, Geneva, 1986.

Dealing with a dunderhead

Job sat on the garbage heap
Mournin', sobbin', mopin',
Till I got him to question God,
And now his eyes are open.

Everything bad that can ever happen has already happened to my husband Job. For a long time he wouldn't talk to me about it.

It didn't start that way. Once upon a time, everything was fine. We were rich. Our lives together were filled with feasting and drinking and giving offerings to God. We continued to be rich. All our wants were taken care of, and we gave what we didn't want to the poor.

But then, his 500 oxen and 500 asses were kidnapped by his enemies. Only one herdsman escaped to tell the tale. It was the first loss Job had ever known.

He was very philosophical about it. He said:

"The Lord gives and the Lord takes away,
Blessed be the name of the Lord."

What a dunderhead!

He sat by himself. He wouldn't talk to anybody.

Then his 7,000 sheep and their shepherds were struck dead by lightning, and only one escaped to tell the tale. And Job moaned:

"The Lord gives and the Lord takes away,
Blessed be the name of the Lord."

What a dunderhead!

He still sat by himself, hugging himself and rocking back and forth in pain. Had one of our children sinned? Was that why God punished him? Couldn't be, because we always made whole offerings to God.

Three bands of Job's enemies raided the camels and captured 3,000 of them, after putting the drivers to the sword, and only one escaped to tell the tale.

Job sat by himself and intoned his comforting little song:

"The Lord gives and the Lord takes away,
Blessed be the name of the Lord."

What a dunderhead!

He wouldn't talk to me. He thought he must have sinned and therefore brought these disasters on himself. It was the first time he had really suffered.

Meantime I was getting really fed up with him. He accepts these bad things too easily. There's no way his bad fortune could be caused by his sin. He doesn't have any sin! He lives a blameless life, does my Job. You just won't find such a good man anywhere in the world. So why doesn't he rebel and get mad at God for the ill fortune that God has dumped on him? He's too patient.

Our seven sons and three daughters were eating and drinking in the eldest brother's house, when suddenly a tornado swept from across the desert. The house collapsed. It fell in on the young people and killed them all. Oh horror!

God, stop this at once! Why are you picking on Job? He doesn't deserve it. But Job sits and moans:

"The Lord gives and the Lord takes away,
Blessed be the name of the Lord."

What a dunderhead!

I can hardly stand to hear him wail. Has he no backbone? He knows he is a good man. So why does he just accept misfortune as though it is what he deserves?

Then, on top of everything else, Job developed running sores and boils from head to foot. I couldn't find him for days. Finally I found him squatting on the garbage dump. He was dirty and worms crawled on his clothes. He had taken a piece of broken pot to scratch himself. Such suffering!

"Job," I screamed. "Job, what on earth are you doing? Show a little backbone," I raged. "Are you still not going to complain to God of your fate? You know you live a good life. Why don't you tell God that? Why do you take it all lying down? Curse God and take the consequences. Talk back."

"You wicked fool of a woman," responded my husband. "If we

accept good from God, should we not also accept the evil?"

Job did not utter one word of rebellion. Nor did he question anything or anyone.

"The Lord gives and the Lord takes away,
Blessed be the name of the Lord."

What a dunderhead! Does he not believe that God is merciful? I was at my wit's end.

When his three good friends heard what was happening, they came and sat with him for a whole week. I don't know what they said. Knowing them, I'm sure they were wrong. But I guess Job must have thought a lot about what I'd said during that week, because at the end of it, he changed his tune.

Not a dunderhead anymore!

He cursed the day of his birth. He peppered God with questions, "Why do the good people suffer? Why is life so bitter? Why are you, God, so unjust?" He showed a little backbone. He was willing to question God. For the first time, he started to really talk **with** God, instead of just sitting and taking it.

No, definitely **not** a dunderhead.

Not only that – he started to get interested in people. He thought it worth arguing with me. He argued with his three friends. He finally made peace with his three friends. He even threw a party and invited all his brothers and sisters and friends, ate with them, and accepted gifts from them. What a party! What a change!

We had seven sons and three daughters again. **Not** a dunderhead.

The most surprising thing was that Job gave our three daughters names that matched their beauty: Bright Day, Cassia (a type of perfume), and Mascara. Job had discovered a new world of beauty and fragrance. Not only that, but my husband made sure our girls would inherit property – something men don't usually do in our tribe.

The best thing of all is that he talks to me now.

Definitely **not** a dunderhead anymore!

The mother of Zebedee's sons

Matthew 20:20–23; Mark 10:39–45; Matthew 27:55–56

Holding the line

In Matthew, the mother of the sons of Zebedee (James and John) is depicted as playing an active part in Jesus' community.

In the first passage, however, she allows herself to be used for her sons' power interests. She is depicted as one who begs Jesus for a favor on her sons' behalf. On the last journey to Jerusalem, she comes with them to ask Jesus if he will promise that her two sons will sit, one at his left and one at his right hand, in his kingdom.

Jesus responds with a question, "Can you drink the cup that I am going to drink?" His question implies struggle, resistance to unjust violence, costly service, and possible death. The woman affirms, with her sons, her readiness to enter into that kind of commitment: "We can."

Read the corresponding passage from Mark for further detail. Here Jesus emphasizes that orders or rank are structures of unjust violence. They are to be resisted. They are to have no place in the community because they express the deep division in society between being "great" or "first" and being served, on the one hand, and being "least" or "last" and serving, on the other. In Jesus' community, authority and power-sharing have to be developed differently so that the community would look different from a society shaped by the dominance of a few.

Traditionally, "serving" in this context has been understood only symbolically; it becomes "being of service." That is the interpretation of the powerful who understand themselves as "being of service." To take the text seriously is to question structures of dominance in a society that maintained, for example, the domination of men over women and that of both men and women owners over slaves.

A modern equivalent would be the structural dominance of our First World over the Two-Thirds World, or the dominance of the relatively wealthy northern and Western churches over their economically impoverished partner churches in developing countries. The text cries out for structural mutuality and reciprocity in human relationships, not just kindness and "being of service" within the unjust structures.

Apparently the mother of the sons of Zebedee entered upon the path of struggle, of resistance to unjust structures, and of costly service, before her sons did. Like the other male disciples, they fled when things became too tough. She stayed with Jesus all through that last agonizing week. She stood with other women under the cross, in solidarity and mutuality with Jesus. She risked the danger to her life from Roman authorities, as did other relatives of crucified persons (Matthew

27:56) by that simple act of solidarity. She knew Jesus would stick by her, even though she was one of the "least," and she reciprocated.

For further reading

Schottroff, Luise. *Lydia's Impatient Sisters: a Feminist Social History of Early Christianity*. Westminster/John Knox, Louisville, KY, 1995

Holding the line

Through thick and thin
We learned to be kin,
Through rain or shine,
We held that line.

I had always loved him. My sons, James and John, tried so hard to follow him. They even left their fishing boats to follow him. They got me interested in him. In fact, I followed him from Galilee and looked after him. I joined Mary of Magdala and some other women to do that. I got to know him well.

The turning point for me was that day we were all on our way to Jerusalem. I didn't really want to ask a favor, but I did it for the sake of my boys. They had always loved rewards and prizes – even when they were little tykes. One year James won a prize for catching the biggest fish in the Sea of Galilee. John was the champion mender of fishing nets, and always won that contest. Now they had begged me to ask for the biggest prize of all. They begged me to ask Jesus if they could have the most important places in his kingdom. So I did.

"You have no idea what you're asking," Jesus replied. "Can you drink the cup that I am going to drink?" He meant, can we share all the suffering and struggle and hard times with him?

"We can," my boys breezily responded.

"I can," I sort of whispered, wondering how I could possibly stick with him. The crowds loved him, but the people in power wanted him out of the way. It would be dangerous to be seen around him.

That final week was terrible. After he was arrested, all his disciples, including my boys, ran away and left him. Even Peter, when he saw his own life was in danger, said he had never known Jesus. At the end, they put a crown of thorns on his head and nailed him to a cross.

But I stayed with him. After all, I had promised. They made fun of him. I stayed with him. The sky became dark. I stayed with him. There was an earthquake and the rocks split open. I was terrified, but I stayed with him. Mary of Magdala held my hands and said we must stay with Jesus, just as he had always stayed with us. That's what "drinking his cup" meant. Even the Roman guards were scared out of their wits.

So we stayed with him. We were a little bit away from the cross, standing on some rocky ground, but we saw it all. We women wailed and cried, sobbed, and hugged each other. But we stayed. Even when the Roman guards noticed us, and could have arrested us just for being there, we stayed. Even when the ninth hour came and Jesus cried out in pain, we stayed.

When a man called Joseph came to claim Jesus' body for burial, we stayed. He took it down from the cross, wrapped it in a cloth, and put it in a cave carved from rock. We stayed to see where the tomb was. Then we prepared spices and ointments. And when the Sabbath Day came we rested.

I'm glad we stayed with him. I knew he would always stay with us too, as he had promised. I wondered how that could be, now that he was in the tomb. But I knew he would keep his promise. Somehow.

Women of the Hebrew Scriptures

Widow of Sidon

I Kings 17:8–24

Learning to trust

Traditionally, the emphasis in this story has been on Elijah as a man of God who bears witness to God's dependability (I Kings 17:23–24). The story is concerned with prophetic recognition and power. A parallel but commonly overlooked theme has been the plight of the widow and her son, who, if they are to believe that God is dependable, have to gamble their lives on their belief.

The conversion scene in 17:17–24 – where the widow calls Elijah "a man of God" – is there to ensure the continuity of Yahweh-worship in Israel. She, a foreign woman, is treated as a sign to God's people.

The widow, along with orphans and sojourners, was among the most vulnerable, most insecure, most dependent in Hebrew society. Her husband is dead; she has no grown son to support her.

The story is about God restoring life, dignity, and a measure of independence to those caught in dependency and powerlessness that has become unbearable. The story focuses on the widow trying to survive with her young son in the midst of severe drought. She herself had few provisions and, of course, no man to provide for her. The story obliquely critiques a social system which sidelines poor women; it highlights God's dependable intervention on behalf of the downtrodden.

She lived in Zarephath, a port city on the coast between Tyre and Sidon. Elijah, who has been camping out beside a brook, comes along and makes what seem like excessive demands on her: water and then cake, served first to him. All she has is a little water, flour, and oil. They are sacramental symbols. In the hands of this widow, they give life to God's anointed prophet. The ensuing miracle reveals that God is dependable, and will provide for her needs in a special way.

Staking her survival on her belief, she shares, and her hospitality is rewarded by the meager supply of grain being continually replenished, and her son being restored to life. The life of a single child becomes a hopeful sign of the fate of the larger body of Israel.

Both miracles have parallels in the Elisha stories of 2 Kings, where the widow's jar of oil keeps overflowing and a dead son is restored to life. They may have been repeated there simply because these are common themes of folklore, expressing God's dependability and the rewards of risking one's life on believing in that dependability.

The widow and prophet were dependent on each other for life. They reconstitute community by assisting each other. The widow is noteworthy for risking her life in response to Elijah's promises about God's dependability.

A parallel story in Luke 7:16 has Jesus similarly resuscitating the son of a widow of Nain. No wonder people called Jesus "another Elijah."

For further reading

Winter, Miriam Therese. *Woman Wisdom: Women of the Hebrew Scriptures: Part One*. Crossroad, NY, 1991, pp. 313 ff.

Bellis, Alice Ogden. *Helpmates, Harlots, Heroes:Women's Stories in the Hebrew Bible*. Westminster/John Knox, Louisville, KY, 1994, pp. 170 ff.

Laffey, Alice, *An Introduction to the Old Testament*, Fortress, Philadelphia, 1988, pp. 134 ff.

Learning to trust

A little oil, a handful of flour –
The widow's dower: Elijah's power.

There was no rain. For some time, Elijah had been living by a stream. He smelled. He was dirty. The ravens fed him, and he drank water from the brook to stay alive.

Then the stream dried up.

But God did not want Elijah to die. So God smiled on him and said to him, "Go to a town called Zarephath, a village of Sidon, and stay there. There is a widow there who will feed you."

Elijah did as he was told. Sure enough, he met a bent-over thin widow who was gathering a few spindly twigs to try to make a fire. She saw this tired, dirty, unshaven man coming toward her.

He spoke just above a whisper, having such a dry mouth. "Please bring me a little water in a pitcher to drink."

As she went to fetch it, he croaked after her, "Bring me, please, a piece of bread as well."

She snapped back angrily, "I have no food to sustain **me**, except the dregs of flour in a jar and a little oil in a flask. Here you find me, gathering two or three sticks to go and cook a last meal for my son and myself before we both die. And you ask me for water and bread?"

Elijah glowered at this uppity woman who flew off the handle just because he had given her instructions. Who did she think she was? He continued to instruct her. "Never fear," he croaked", go and do as you intend. But first make me some pita bread from what you have and bring it out to me. After that you can make something for your son and for yourself."

The widow was used to being told what to do by men. But this man was more impossible than any she had ever met. She had practically nothing. How did he expect her small bit of food to feed them both?

"Your flask of oil and your jar of flour will not run out until God sends more rain on the land," Elijah promised.

God smiled at this. God was happy that Elijah had so much trust.

Despite her anger, the widow wanted to trust this grubby tired man who told her that God wouldn't let them starve to death. So she went and did as Elijah said.

Lo and behold, there was food and drink for her, for her son, and for Elijah for a long long time. So, thought the widow to herself, God really can and does provide.

But the drought didn't end. And it got so hot she could have fried an egg on a rock – if she had an egg to fry. And then the widow's son fell sick. He grew worse and worse until he stopped breathing. The widow lit into Elijah: "It's all your fault. What made you come into our lives anyway? You came here to cause the death of my son."

"Give me your son," said Elijah gently, because he had learned to care deeply about this woman and her child. He took the boy from the arms of his mother and carried him up to his own small room on the roof top, and laid him on his own bed. Then he raged at God. "God, is this how you look after this widow? Why have you been so cruel to her son? She has nothing in life except her son."

Then he breathed three times into the child's mouth and cried out, "Let the breath of life return to this child's body."

After a while the boy revived and sat up. Elijah lifted him up and took him down from the roof of the house, and gave him back to his mother. "Look," he said, "your son is alive."

"Now I know you are a man of God," she cried", and we can depend on God's promises. Now I have hope again."

And God smiled.

Solomon

I Kings 3:16–28

The mystery of the true mother

This story concerns the dilemma of two prostitutes. It is about the willingness of one of them to forego strict justice to preserve the life of her infant. Read it in 1 Kings 3:16–28.

The story is usually interpreted to establish the wisdom of Solomon (whose name means "peace"). In that sense, this fictional folk tale casts the two competing women merely as a foil for the wisdom of a male.

However, there can be another viewpoint, particularly when one wonders how it was that "wise" Solomon "lost" the kingdom David had built up.

Prostitutes were – and still are – stereotyped by society as unreliable and uncaring. They were, and are, commonly despised. Indeed, some rabbis of former days questioned whether these two women could really have been prostitutes. "If they had really been prostitutes," the rabbis argued, "they would not have cared enough for their children to go to court." The cultural norm was that a woman was man's property, along with everything else he owned. Even today we speak of the "master" bedroom as though it "belongs" to the man.

Prostitutes, because they didn't belong to any man, were a real threat to patriarchy. This "outsider" role of those whose sexuality is not controlled by either father or husband generates an expectation that all one would hear from such women would be lies.

This assumption is challenged by the response of one of the two women, the mother, who "because her heart (womb) yearned for her child," put the life of her baby above egoism, possessiveness, and even justice. The rabbinical commentary on this story says that "some rabbis claim that even a prostitute can have compassion for her own child." Not only does the tale subvert the societal stereotype of prostitutes, but it is a metaphor for the compassion of God, who always chooses life over death, mercy over legalism.

Phyllis Trible describes this ancient story as a paradigm for understanding a particular Biblical metaphor – linking the womb of women with the compassion of God. In Hebrew, the sound of the two words are similar, and the use of one would, to the fine-tuned ear of the Israelites, set off echoes of the other. The Hebrew word in the singular means "womb"; in the plural it means "compassion," thus linking the two. In some instances biblically, God is given a womb (a feminine attribute certainly!) which emphasizes God's compassion. Isaiah 46:3–4 speaks of Israel as a load "carried by me (God) from the womb...I have made you and I will bear the burden, I will carry you and bring you to safety." An awareness of this metaphor led me to fashion a benediction that starts this way, "God, who has carried us in the womb from the beginning..."

For further reading

Trible, Phyllis. *God and the Rhetoric of Sexuality.* Fortress, Philadelphia, 1978, Chapter 2.

Williams, Michael. *The Storyteller's Companion to the Bible,* Vol. IV. Abingdon Press, Nashville, TN, 1993.

Newsom, Carol A. and Sharon H. Ringe, eds. *The Women's Bible Commentary.* Westminster/John Knox, Louisville, 1992, pp. 100 ff.

The mystery of the true mother

Who is the mother true?
They asked the king so wise.
The loving one – she knew!
The other told great lies.

The little legs of the howling newborn baby stuck out of the blanket cradled by a woman. Another woman grabbed the baby from her, and spat her words at the first woman. "This is my baby. Give her to me."

"She's mine, you sneaky snake pit."

"She not, you slimy hag."

"She's mine. Don't take a fit!"

"Go rot. You great big bag."

Back and forth they screeched while the infant screamed with fright.

They both claimed the baby. Neither of them had a husband to defend their claim. They were prostitutes.

They asked King Solomon to decide. Each woman presented her case.

"She's mine, you tricky liar."

"She's mine, you mucky sleeze."

"She's mine, she's not for hire."

"Come on, she's mine, oh jeez!"

The first woman, holding the baby, told the king they shared the same house. Both had given birth to a baby within a few days of each other. During the night, she said, the second woman's baby died because she lay on it.

At this, the second woman made a grab for the baby, who screamed even louder: "Ow. Ow."

"When I woke up," said the first woman, "I noticed the baby beside me in my bed was not my baby."

"That's a filthy lie if I ever heard one," screeched the second woman.

"Who's telling lies?" jibed the first woman. "During the night that sleezy lump lay on her baby and suffocated it. When she found out, she took my baby from my side while I was asleep, and laid it in her bed, putting her dead baby in my bed."

"You mucky sleeze. I spit on you." And the second woman did, as she snatched the baby from the arms of the first woman. More howls from the baby, who was now beside herself: "Ow-ow-ow."

"Give her back, you schlunk," howled the first woman. She wrenched the poor baby from the arms of the other woman.

So it went. Back and forth. Back and forth. No one had been in the house when the babies were born. Neither woman had a husband. There was no one to support their stories.

In short order, Solomon got tired of listening to them fight with each other. He ordered his servants to bring him a sword. "Cut the baby in two and give half to one, and half to the other," he directed, disgusted with their squabbling.

At this, the first woman, who was the real mother of the living baby, gave an anguished wail: "Don't kill my baby. I'd rather that scum have it," she blurted, pointing to the other woman. "Whatever you do, don't kill my baby."

"Cut her in two. Cut her in two. Let neither of us have the baby," said the second woman, who was not the mother of the living baby.

"She's mine, you sneaky snake pit."

"She's not, you slimy hag."

"She's mine, don't take a fit!"

"Go rot, you great big bag."

What was Solomon to do? Finally he spoke. "Do not kill the baby. Give her to the first woman, who is the real mother. I know she is, because her heart longs to let her baby live. Justice says that she should have her own baby back. But she would rather let go of justice for herself, so that her baby will live."

The true mother burst into tears with relief.

The sneaky snake pit cuddled the baby and smirked.

The courtiers were amazed.

The people were astonished.

And the baby quit screaming and gurgled with delight. She was going to live!

Julia's story

(Based on a true story told to the author in 1984)

I'll never forget the day I picked up the phone and heard a voice on the telephone ask to speak to Julia.

"This is Julia speaking," I answered.

"Julia, this is your mother, phoning from Switzerland." I heard muffled sobs. I was so shocked I couldn't respond.

"Are you still there, Julia?" the urgent voice repeated. "Are you still there?"

"Yes, I am," I managed to blurt out. "Where are you? How did you find me?" I was beginning to tremble with excitement and delight. Could this really be my birth mother?

"I'm phoning from Switzerland," she said again. "I wanted to be sure I have really found you again. Dear, dear Julia. I love you and have found you again. That's all that matters."

"But how did you find me? I've dreamed about you finding me, but thought it would never happen. How did you find me again?" I pleaded. I was half laughing and half crying with excitement.

"It was through the churches. But I'll tell you the whole story when I see you," she replied.

"When's that? When's that?" I eagerly asked.

"In two days. I'm coming to Argentina in two days' time to see you again, and to tell you all about it. It's such a long painful story".

Then my adoptive mom got on the phone. There were more exclamations, tears, and disbelief. I knew that Rosemarie, my adoptive mom, had been a neighbor of my birth mother. She had talked about her a lot. My birth mother gave Rosemarie all the flight details for her arrival in Argentina.

We were right up at the front of the crowd welcoming travelers at the airport. I had made a sign with my name on it with the letters "JULIA" spelled out in black firm lettering and I held it high. I still wondered if it would happen. After ten years!

A tall slim woman with red hair spotted me at once, and made a beeline for me. She glanced at Rosemarie but didn't hesitate. Her eyes danced and she saw my eyes light up at the same time. It was if a fire was lit inside us, shining out of our eyes. Without words we hugged and kissed and smiled and hugged and kissed again. We held each other so tightly I thought my ribs would crack.

"Julia, is it really you?" she murmured through her tears.

"Mom, I knew it was you 'cause you have red hair," I stuttered through my tears. We were both wiping our eyes and blowing our noses.

"Rosemarie, dear," my mom murmured as my two moms hugged each other. All three of us encircled each other's waists.

Later, we heard the whole story from my birth mother.

"Julia, your daddy and I lived in Argentina during the 1970s. Many people were becoming very poor, and we decided to do what we could to help them. The government told the soldiers to arrest anyone who was helping the poor, because they wanted to keep all the country's money for themselves.

"One day, your daddy went to work but he never came home. He just 'disappeared' off the face of the earth. I was expecting you at the time. I was so happy when you were born. But I was afraid the soldiers would take you from me as punishment for your daddy and me working with the poor. So I phoned my neighbor Rosemarie and gave you to her for safekeeping. I hoped it would soon be safe for me to look after you myself.

"Sure enough, the soldiers came and arrested me. I was put into prison. The prison was damp and cold and the food was terrible. Some of the mothers in prison had their newborn babies taken from them and adopted into the soldier's families. It was so sad and hopeless.

"When Rosemarie asked the police about returning you to me in prison, the police said they certainly didn't have me in their prison. What a lie!

"I was in prison quite a long time. When I got out, I discovered Rosemarie had moved, and taken you along with them. I didn't know where you were. I searched and searched. I asked a lot of people, although that was a dangerous thing to do, because they might have been friends of the police and reported me. I never saw you again until now – ten years later!

"I started my work with the poor again, but was afraid of being arrested. So I left Argentina and went to Switzerland. I married again and had your little sister, Maria – "

I was amazed. I had a little sister! A sister I had never even heard of!

" – but I never, never forgot you, even though I wondered if you were dead. I kept talking about you a lot and wondered what you looked like. I asked the churches in Switzerland if they could help me find you, my 'lost' daughter Julia. The only thing I could tell them about you was that you would probably have red hair. And you do," she said, stroking my flaming hair.

"They said it was like searching for a needle in a haystack but they would try.

"After ten years, the churches located Rosemarie here who still lives in Argentina, and has adopted you. I'm happy your mother and daddy are going to keep you living with them. It would be cruel to take you away from them after all those years. But never forget that you are my own daughter and I love you very much."

"I'm glad you never forgot me," I said.

"How could I forget my own child?" my birth mom asked, giving me another hug. "I kept talking about you as though I would find you some day even when I didn't know if that was possible. I love you."

"All that time," I said, "I lived with my mommy and dad that had adopted me. I knew they used to be neighbors of yours, 'cause they talked about you. They love me a lot, too."

I still live with my adoptive parents, but I see my birth mother whenever I like. She loves me too. It's fantastic that I have two mothers, both of whom love me very much.

I often lie awake at night, looking at the stars in the sky, thinking how amazing they are. But when I think of having two moms who love me very much, I know that my life is more amazing than even the stars!

True wisdom

There was once a king who had three daughters. As he was getting older the king wanted to divide his kingdom among them, but he didn't know which princess should rule after him upon his death. So he sent them all out into the world, to prove themselves worthy of the crown.

The first daughter traveled to many distant kingdoms. Everywhere tales of her beauty went before her, and everywhere she was met with rich presents. She had a knack for business, and shrewdly bought and sold many things. She returned home a wealthy woman with beautiful possessions.

The second daughter studied many arts, until she mastered the secret of spinning the most wondrous cloths. She spun fabric that looked as though it were made of snowflakes, clothes that looked seamed of moonbeams, tapestries that gleamed from within, as if from sunlight. She too returned home a rich woman.

The third daughter began her travels uncertain of where her destiny lay. She read many books and maps and studied the law and languages of the land. For months she journeyed, listening and learning until she understood all the peoples of her father's kingdom. At last she returned home. There she sought counsel of her closest friend, a young man who loved learning just as much as she did. They talked and talked for many days and nights, until they realized they were deeply in love. With the blessing of the king, the princess and the young man were soon married.

When it came time for the king to divide his kingdom, he gave one third of his wealth to his eldest daughter, for she knew how to manage riches. To the second daughter he also gave one third, for her skill had taught her to appreciate good things.

But it was to the third princess that he gave his crown and his lands, for she understood the peoples of his kingdom, both near and far. And a kingdom must be ruled with wisdom and love.

The princess became queen and her husband became king. Together they ruled wisely and well for many years.

With acknowledgments to Betty Lehrman, a professional storyteller from Framingham, Mass. From *The Storytellers Companion to the Bible: Old Testament Women,* ed. Michael Williams, Vol. IV, Abingdon Press, Nashville, 1993.

The wisdom of the young judge

Deut. 16:18–20

Before you read this story, read the biblical verses Deuteronomy 16:18–20. They deal with justice. One of the first things God did after the Jews reached the promised land was to have judges appointed. Jews have always known that justice, peace, and truth are interdependent. They are the first priority for a sustainable society and world.

Jews have also been telling stories for a long, long time. Studying the weekly portion of the Torah continues to be an important part of Jewish education. This story, from Jewish folklore, is rooted in and based on the weekly verses (*sidrah*) cited above.

The story is intended to engage young listeners in a study of the Torah. It imagines that the young child playing the part of a judge is a girl, to emphasize that some Hebrew judges (both then and now) are women.

The wisdom of the young judge

Joseph was a dealer in spices. In the next shop there was a man who sold olive oil. His name was Meir. They had operated their shops next door to one another for 20 years. But lately, Joseph noticed that more people were buying from Meir than from him. He knew Meir was making a lot of money. He became jealous.

So one day, he ran out into the street shouting, "I've been robbed. Can't anyone help me?"

"Who robbed you and what has been stolen?" asked some of the curious crowd who were on the street.

"All the money from today's sales has been stolen. One hundred gold coins. I am sure it was my neighbor Meir. His business has not been very good lately and he is jealous of my success."

And that is how Joseph accused his neighbor Meir.

When Meir was arrested, he accused Joseph of lying. The Judge didn't know what to do. Neither Meir or Joseph had any proof that the money was his. How was the Judge to decide wisely?

The Judge said he would decide the next day. In the meantime he went for a walk, turned a corner, and found some children playing in a school yard. The students had decided to play judge. All the children had, of course, heard about the case of Joseph and Meir. One of the students declared herself as judge. Two decided they would be the lawyers. The other two played the part of Meir and Joseph, hurling insults at each other.

"You're a thief. You stole my money," said one.

"No, you're the thief. You're jealous of me."

"Knothead!" said one.

"Snake's tail!" yelled the other.

Back and forth the accusations went. Finally the young judge said she was ready to give a judgment. "Bring me a bucket of water," she commanded. "Put the coins in the water. If the coins belong to the olive oil merchant, the oil from the coins will be seen in the water. If there is no oil, then they must belong to the spice merchant."

The next day the Judge stood in the courtroom and asked for a bucket of water. He placed the coins in the water just as he had seen the children do the day before. Sure enough, they were full of oil.

"Give the coins back to their rightful owner, to Meir," he ordered.

And Joseph was taken from the courtroom and put in jail for the attempted theft of Meir's money.

Everyone whispered about how wise the Judge was. But the Judge knew who was truly wise. He motioned to someone standing near the door. A very nervous little girl stood there.

"Here is your wise judge," announced the Judge. "She has taught me that wisdom is not always determined by age, nor justice by the person with a title."

The little girl, whose name was Deborah, herself grew up to be a Judge. As she grew, so did her wisdom.

Adapted with permission from Hebrew folklore in *Sidrah Stories: A Torah Companion* by Steven Rosman, UAHC Press, NY, 1989, p. 158.

The woman and the dove
Deuteronomy 30:19

This story is rooted in Deuteronomy 30:19. Read this verse before proceeding. The verse emphasizes choices and the consequence of free will that we all have. We have the power to bring life or death.

The woman and the dove

There was once a rabbi who was so wise there was no question he could not answer. People came from far and wide to ask him questions. Everyone adored him.

Everyone, that is, except one. Her name was Athaliah, and she was ten years old. She had always been a bit of a rebel. When her grandma offered her a bedtime of either eight or nine o'clock, she always suggested ten. When Grandpa explained why the sky was blue, she wanted to know why it's red at sunset. When her mother asked her if she preferred rice or pasta for supper, she always suggested chicken.

She planned to ask the rabbi a question he could not answer. Then she would become known as wiser than the rabbi!

She began to carry out her plan, traveling to the village where the rabbi lived. She asked the rabbi, "Who, with one blow, killed one-quarter of the people in the world?"

No one spoke as they awaited the rabbi's answer. "When Cain murdered Abel, he destroyed one-quarter of the world's population," answered the rabbi in a quiet voice.

Athaliah was angry. So she came back the next day to see if she could trap the rabbi with a question that couldn't be answered.

"Rabbi" she asked, "it is written that Noah gathered all the creatures of the earth with him in the ark. Yet there was one creature that did not come aboard. Which was that?"

There was a long silence. "Once again you have challenged me," said the rabbi to Athaliah. "In this case, the only creatures that were not aboard the ark during the Flood had to be the fish that swam alongside it all the 40 days and 40 nights."

Athaliah flushed. She worked hard on a third question she might pose the next day.

The next day she went to the rabbi and reached into a bag she had brought. With two hands hidden behind her back, she approached the rabbi.

"Rabbi," she said, "I am holding a dove in my hands. Can you tell me if it is alive or dead?"

Athaliah thought she had made up a wicked scheme. If the rabbi replied that the bird was dead, Athaliah would simply open her hands to show everyone a live dove. If the rabbi said the bird was alive, then Athaliah would close her hands around the dove and smother it, showing everyone a dead bird. "There is no way the rabbi can see through this puzzle," thought Athaliah.

Although only a few moments passed, it seemed like forever before the rabbi spoke.

"Athaliah, you have given us a very difficult puzzle. In your hands you hold a life. Choose wisely what you will do with it. The answer to your puzzle, Athaliah, lies in your hands, not mine."

Adapted with permission from Hebrew folklore in *Sidrah Stories: A Torah Companion* by Steven Rosman, UAHC Press, NY, 1989, p. 169.

Lot's wife

Genesis 19:24–27; Luke 17:32

The woman who looked back

The story is very ancient and should not be taken literally, although it conveys a profound truth.

The story of Lot's wife is likely a tale told to account for some unusual salt formations in the south end of the Dead Sea. But why is it Lot's wife, and not Lot, who turns back and is destroyed? Lot, after all, was not such an enviable character. When he and Abraham divided up the land, Lot grabbed the most fertile part. He was willing to turn his daughters over to gang rape to spare the strangers who had sought hospitality from him. Lot is not condemned for this action, nor for his later drunken incestuous relations with his daughters. I leave it to you to conclude as to what that says about the situation of women.

Throughout the Bible, Sodom remains a metaphorical punishment for sin. The word "sodomy," derived from this chapter, refers specifically to forced rape by anal intercourse, without consent, whether between heterosexual couples or otherwise. To use the word sodomy for other forms of sexual intimacy misrepresents this ancient text. It also ignores the meaning given to this ancient city by Jesus and many of the great prophets of Israel, all of whom equated the symbol of Sodom with punishment of a great variety of sins, none of them sexual. Ezekiel 16:49–50, for example, spells out the sins for which Sodom was destroyed: out of their immense wealth, comfort, and ease, they never shared with the poor and wretched. Isaiah 1:10 and 17 links Sodom with the need to pursue justice and champion the oppressed, and warns against sacrifice without justice. Amos 4:1 and 11 speaks to "those who oppress the poor and crush the destitute... I brought destruction amongst you as God destroyed Sodom." Lamentations 4:4 speaks of "the sucking infant's tongue cleaving to its palate from thirst. Young children beg for bread, but no one offers them a crumb. The punishment of my people is worse than the chastisement of Sodom."

The truth that we are to remember has to do mainly with looking back selfishly, with enviously remembering the riches and luxury that were exclusively ours, wealth that tends to cut us off from a future of being truly alive. When Lot's wife looks back, her life ends.

Jesus is reported in Luke as saying, "Remember Lot's wife?" This saying occurs in the context of Jesus teaching that "Whoever seeks to gain his life, will lose it" (Luke 17:32–33).

For further reading

Bellis, Alice Ogden. *Helpmates, Harlots, Heroes: Women's Stories in the Hebrew Bible*. Westminster/John Knox Press, Louisville, KY, 1994, pp. 79–80.

Weems, Renita J. *Just a Sister Away: A Womanist Vision of Women's Relationships in the Bible*. Lura Media, San Diego, CA, 1988, p.129.

Brash, Alan. *Facing our Differences: The Churches and their Gay and Lesbian Members*. World Council of Churches, Geneva, 1995.

The woman who looked back

Lot had lots of lovely things
To show to one and all,
But not a thing to give away
Was Lot's wife's great downfall.

Lot was a wealthy man. When he and Uncle Abraham came to settle in the fertile plain of Jordan, Abraham offered Lot a choice of which fields he would like for himself. Lot chose the most fertile ones, and left the poorer ones to his uncle.

Lot settled in the city of Sodom. Over time, he became wealthy.
He owned hundreds of sheep,
thousands of calves,
tens of thousands of cows.
His wife prepared huge feasts, and served
baskets of figs and oranges,
cartloads of pomegranates and lemons,
tents full of lamb and beef.
Everyone ate until they could eat no more.
They drank until they could drink no more.

Lot and his wife sold their grain, their beef, their lamb at a high price.

They bought everything in sight.

glittering jewels,
shiny smooth fabrics,
rustling silks,
cloaks the colors of the rainbow.

They built a monstrous house, made of the finest stone, so large that even Lot's wife had never been in all of the rooms.

But Lot's wife did not share any of her wealth with the poor.

One day God looked on Sodom and became angry. The people of the city were treating each other brutally and cruelly. Many of them were doing wicked things to each other. The rich never shared with the wretched people.

So God decided to rain fire and brimstone on the cities, on the valley, on all the people of the cities, and on everything that grew on the ground.

Two angels advised Lot and his wife and daughters to leave at once.

"Run as fast as you can," they said. "Leave at once and don't stop to take anything with you."

Lot did, and he took his daughters with him to live in a cave.

His wife started out with them. But at the last moment she stopped. She turned and looked back at all that had been hers. She thought of the

hundreds of sheep,
thousands of calves,
tens of thousands of cows.

She thought of

the baskets of figs and oranges,
the cartloads of pomegranates and lemons,
the tents full of lamb and beef.

She thought of

the glittering jewels,
the shiny smooth fabrics,
the rustling silks,

the cloaks the colors of the rainbow.

She thought of her monstrous house, made of the finest stone, so large that even she had never been in all of the rooms.

All that was being left behind. She didn't want to think about the future. It was too bleak and empty. So she looked back and stayed looking back, thinking of all that she had lost and refused to share.

God frowned.

And she's still there. She remained frozen in place forever like a pillar of salt in the flats, her life over.

Why did I look back?

But Lot's wife behind him looked back, and she became a pillar of salt. (Gen. 19:26).

In the ancient land of Canaan was the city of Sodom where Lot lived. A very mixed group of people lived there (Genesis 15:18–21), not all of them worshipers of Yahweh, the God of the Hebrews. The Bible points to a variety of religious beliefs held by different groups of people. How might Lot's wife have felt about them, and about leaving those folk she had come to know so well? That is the context of this story/poem. You may want to read it as is, or fashion a story in your own words.

The story/poem is written by Dr. Stanley J. Samartha of India. He also lives in a country with a wide variety of religious communities. Hindus are a majority, with Muslims coming next. Christians are a minority. Most of his life has been dedicated to enabling different religious communities to encounter one another in creative ways, instead of stereotyping others and labeling them "bad" because they are different from us. For some years, he headed up the World Council of Churches' program on "Dialogue with Other Faiths." The aim was not to convert the other to Christianity, but to recognize the common pilgrimage toward authentic community and fullness of life that we are on together, even though we recognize the vast differences we have. And the Christian is called to love, above all.

Canada is itself now a very multifaith community, and this story is applicable to our situation, as it is to any situation of diversity between people. It suggests in the last two lines that Lot's wife would rather give up her own salvation, her own "safety," than betray and desert her neighbors.

How many of us have that strong a commitment to our neighbors (whether they be Hindu, Muslim, or any other) that the Christian faith demands?

Why did I look back?

by Stanley Samartha

I was afraid of the two strangers
who came to our house last evening.
They said "we" were good.
But "they," our neighbors, were bad.
Lot was so pleased
That he did a big "namasthe"* to them
And asked me to prepare a feast.
Lot said they were angels, but I was afraid of them.
Their faces were cold, their looks harsh, and their eyes were burning with anger.

Why did I look back?

I was angry at Lot.
When the men surrounded our house
and wanted the strangers to come out,
Lot offered to send our virgin daughters to them.
But both the girls were engaged to be married.
I was angry. Very angry. Outraged.
I pushed them into the little storeroom at the back.
I stood guard over against it. Over my dead body.
When those men wanted men, why send girls to them?
Why didn't Lot himself go?

Why didn't the two angels go?
That would have been an angelic happening.

Why did I look back?

Because my neighbors were out there.
When, during the birth of my first child, I cried out in pain,
The women were there.
They held my hands, wiped my brow,
Gave me water to drink. And when the baby was born,
they bathed it and put it to my breast.

And where was Lot?
He was out in the fields praying to his God.

When my little girl hit her foot against a stone
And broke her toenail,
My neighbors came with some crushed leaves,
And put them in her tea. My daughter smiled through tears.

And where was Lot?
He was out in the fields praying to his God.

You say only the women were good, but the men were bad?
When there was no water for three days
And my children were crying,
My neighbor's husband walked three miles to get water.
And then he gave us some.

Why did I look back?

Because I wanted to perish with my neighbor
Rather than be saved without them.

Quoted by Rev. Sun Ai Lee Park, at The First Asian Women's Conference on Interfaith Dialogue, 1989 Kuala Lumpur, Malaysia, and printed with the permission from *author, Stanley Samartha.*

* namasthe is a Hindu greeting and welcome.

Potiphar's wife

Genesis 39:7–9, 12, and 19

Soon forgotten

The story of Potiphar's wife is an unlikely tale, historically. It is often compared to the first episode of "The Tale of the Two Brothers," an Egyptian tale, which closely parallels Genesis 39:7–20. In each case, the upright person who works for a superior is approached by the superior, rejects the approach, and is then accused of rape. The upright person faces an impossible dilemma: he will be destroyed if he accepts the proposition made to him; he will equally be destroyed if he does not accept it.

Yet the folk-tale motif in this story points to eventual long-term positive results for the hero, Joseph. Potiphar's wife is depicted as aggressive, independent, and a stereotypically sexually-potent evil foreign woman. She is portrayed as disloyal to her husband, and quick to seek satisfaction in forbidden places. Why is she portrayed in this way?

Remember, a tale is told to make a point, not to convey history. Potiphar's wife is a foil for the hero. Her destructive actions, a common motif in the classic quest for hero, usually resulted in a positive transformation for the male hero – in this case, Joseph.

Let's explore that theme a little further.

The actions of this apparently vindictive woman moved a young man, Joseph, from his safe situation as a servant into virtual exile (prison) and then into rebirth at a much higher stratum of society (second-in-command in all Egypt). Is it possible, then, to view this negatively portrayed woman as effecting a positive change? She was a catalyst for long-term gain for the model hero, Joseph.

In folklore using this motif, the change carried ramifications that extended far beyond the hero himself to the community of which he was a part. For Joseph, the charge of rape led to prison, not death. His interpretation of dreams in prison led to Pharaoh summoning him to a position in Pharaoh's household much higher than the position he once held in Potiphar's household. It is Joseph, freed from prison, whom the king eventually chooses to be his national administrator. From this position, Joseph was later able provide salvation for his own family when the famine-starved Israelites sought grain in Egypt (Genesis 41:37–46:7). Set in this fuller context, it becomes obvious that the apparently negative effect of Potiphar's wife's accusation actually resulted in Joseph being empowered to help his own family and ensure the continuation of the Israelite people.

This story emphasizes that everything to do with Joseph prospers because God is with him. In that sense, it is a parallel to the story of Susanna, although the gender of accusers and accused is reversed. Her story is undoubtedly modeled after this earlier one. Is it possible to view the negatively portrayed elders as effecting a positive change for the heroine? Despite the unjust charges against Susanna, truth prevails; hypocrisy is punished; she is vindicated.

For further reading

Day, Peggy. *Gender and Difference in Ancient Israel.* Fortress Press, Minneapolis, 1989.

Newsom, Carol A. and Sharon H. Ringe, eds. *The Women's Bible Commentary.* Westminster/John Knox Press, Louisville, 1992, pp. 24 ff.

Soon forgotten

She doesn't have a name.
She's made to take the blame.
Joseph went to jail;
Turns out he won't need bail.

A long long time ago, there was a handsome good-looking young man whose name was Joseph. He had been sold as a slave, in a foreign land called Egypt, to Potiphar, one of Pharaoh's men.

Joseph was a good servant. He looked after Potiphar's property very well. Everything in Potiphar's house prospered under Joseph's care. His fields grew lots of grain. His palm trees became mightier and taller than any others in Egypt. His coconuts gave the richest and juiciest milk of any coconuts in the area. His horses were well groomed and always ready when they were needed.

Potiphar was so pleased with Joseph that he gave him a better job – to be Potiphar's personal, private, servant. Joseph laid out his master's clothing. He was in charge of Potiphar's investments. He did the details of seating guests at dinner parties. He decided what flowers to plant in the gardens. And he did much much more.

Joseph was careful to listen to what Potiphar wanted. He knew what his master thought was funny. He knew what his master thought was important. And above all, he knew what habits, likes, and dislikes Potiphar had. The only thing Potiphar himself paid any attention to was the food he ate. Some said that Joseph knew more about Potiphar than Potiphar knew about himself!

After some time, Potiphar's wife noticed Joseph. She thought him very handsome. And besides, he was much younger than her husband. She knew he would have to obey any command she gave, and she was terribly bored. Poptiphar barely noticed her anymore – he was so busy being busy.

So she decided to order Joseph to do what **she** wanted. "Come and lie with me," she ordered him, stretching luxuriously on her silken pillows.

Joseph knew what Potiphar's wife wanted. But he refused her. He said, "Think of my master. He trusts me with everything that he has. He has appointed me as second-in-command. He has kept nothing of his from me, except you, because you are his wife. How can I possibly do what you ask and not know I shame him and myself?"

Every day, Potiphar's wife tried again.

"Come and sit beside me, Joseph. A little closer."

But Joseph said no.

"Come for a walk in the garden with me, Joseph."

But Joseph said no.

"I am eating alone tonight. Join me."

But Joseph said no.

One day he came to the house to do chores when no other servants were around. Potiphar's wife was waiting for him. She caught him by his cloak and urged him, "Come and lie with me."

Joseph said no.

But she said yes, yes, and tried to drag him with her by his cloak.

He broke away. He ran out of the house, leaving his cloak in her hands.

When the men of the house came home, she waved the cloak at

them. “Look at this!” she said in a loud voice. “My husband has brought in a Hebrew slave to make fun of us. He came in here to lie with me but I screamed at the top of my lungs. When he heard me scream he got frightened, left his cloak in my hands, and ran off.”

Joseph was nowhere to be seen.

Later that night, when Potiphar came home, she repeated her story to him. “That Hebrew slave you brought to our house has been trying to make a fool of me. He wanted me to lie with him. When I screamed for help and called out, he left his cloak in my hands and ran off.”

She knew she had to accuse Joseph in order to appear innocent herself.

Potiphar was furious. He ground his teeth. His face turned red with anger. How could Joseph betray him in such a way? He sent his guards immediately. They arrested Joseph and put him in the Round Tower prison. He had no chance to defend himself. He had no chance to explain that he knew what Potiphar’s wife wanted, but he had said no.

Joseph was as good a prisoner as he had been a servant. After a while he was put in charge of all the prisoners in the Round Tower. He became famous for his gift of interpreting dreams. He even interpreted some dreams for the Pharaoh, the ruler of the whole of Egypt. Pharaoh released him from prison and made him second-in-command for all of Egypt. He became a very important person, remembered by many with admiration.

As for Potiphar’s wife, she was soon forgotten.

Adam and Eve

Genesis chapters 1–3

Mainly the male version

The first three chapters of Genesis were not the first Bible stories to be written, although they are the opening chapters in the Bible. These creation stories were actually written after the Exodus event, to provide a background, a wide canvas, for the subsequent stories of Israel and her people and their destiny. Genesis attempts to describe the origin of the cosmos and its first inhabitants. It unfolds the life stories of an ancient people and sets their origin and destiny in the context of the very creation of the universe itself.

There are two Creation myths in Genesis, in 1:1–2:4a, and 2:4b–3:24. Myth, a form of story, is not history. It is a bearer and creator of culture. It is not true in the usual sense in which we use that word (that is, nobody was there writing it all down as it took place). But it conveys profound truth. It is a story of what never was, but always is. It establishes beliefs, defines rituals, and determines social and moral behavior. Myth opens up depths of reality otherwise closed to us.

Genesis 1 emphasizes the orderliness and goodness of God's Creation. In this sophisticated story, human beings are created last – the crown of creation. Genesis 1:27 says: "So God created humankind (*adam*) in his image, in the image of God he created them; male and female he created them." There is not a hint of one being superior to the other.

The second but earlier story (Genesis 2–3) is the familiar one of Adam and Eve. They should not be understood as historic individuals, for they represent "humankind" and "mother of the living."

Genesis 2 and 3 has traditionally been interpreted to underline women's nature as the sexual seductress and bearer of "original sin" – although this weighty accusation is not stated anywhere in the text. What it does seem to do is grant divine sanction to men's domination of women.

Surprisingly, the creation stories in Genesis are not referred to and reworked as major themes by later writers in the Hebrew Bible, the way the Exodus is. In the time between the writing of the Old and New Testaments, however, the story of Adam and Eve began to be used by writers of extra biblical material. Eve began to surface as the origin of all sin and sexuality, and this emphasis was picked up in the New Testament in passages such as 1 Timothy 2:13–14. Art and literature (Milton's *Paradise Lost,* for example) reinforced the notion of woman's sin.

I base my "fanciful myth" – my retelling of the story – on the work of two researchers: Hebrew scholar David Freedman and Christian scholar Carol Meyers.

Freedman proposes a different translation for the word rendered "helper"(Genesis 2:18b). He translates the Hebrew word *ezer* as "power": power to rescue, to save, to be strong. The second Hebrew word *kenegdo* appears only once in the Bible, and means "equal." The Hebrew phrase *ezer kenegdo* came to be translated "a helpmate fit for him," reading a later social situation back into an earlier text. But Freedman says the phrase *ezer kenegdo* really means "a power equal" to Adam. Eve was not intended to be Adam's rescuer, or helper, claims Freedman. She was intended to be a strength equivalent to Adam.

This harmonizes with Genesis 1's "God made them in the image of God." The New English Bible (1970) translates the word as "partner." "Male and female he created them" does not imply the superiority of either.

Contemporary scholar Carol Meyers rejects traditional interpretations that view sin as the central theme of Genesis 3. She thinks the stories (similar to myths of other cultures) are there to explain why certain human conditions exist: for example, how life became so disharmonious. Eve has a prominent role – she is curious, active, articulate, and sees that the tree is good for making one wise. Adam is passive and silent. The snake is a trickster, overturning the status quo. Perhaps eating the apple was a necessary disobedience, because freedom is the one thing that God could not build directly into the universe. In this interaction, woman helps to generate a new, challenging life beyond Eden.

For further reading

Bellis, Alice Ogden. *Helpmates, Harlots, Heroes: Women's Stories in the Hebrew Scriptures*. Westminster/John Knox Press, Louisville, KY, 1994, pp. 45 ff., esp. p. 54 (summary of Freedman) and p. 58 ff. (summary of Meyers).

Freedman, R. David. "Woman, a Power Equal to Man," *Biblical Archeological Review*, Jan/Feb 1983, Vol. IX No. 1, pp. 56-58.

Meyers, Carol L. *Discovering Eve: Ancient Israelite Women in Context*. Oxford University Press, NY, 1988.

Mainly the male version

a fanciful tale by Pheobe Willetts

A game for two voices:

(1) Adam and Eve and Pinch Me Tight
Went down to the river to bathe;
Adam and Eve were drownd-ed
Now who do you think was saved?
(2) That's easy! Pinch Me Tight!
(1) Okay.
(2) Ow!

It was a lovely spring morning in Paradise. Adam was taking his usual nap after lunch while Eve was wondering about something. She was curious about everything. "How long will it take to populate the world?" she asked, scratching her nose.

"You look beautiful when you scratch your nose," said Adam. The flowers nodded and smiled at him as they knew they had been created to give pleasure. The lambs were snuggling up to the lions as everyone was still vegetarian. Shrewdy the snake sunned himself contentedly, not having any idea of the blame that was soon going to be loaded onto his narrow shoulders.

Then one day, a quarrel erupted and everyone began blaming everyone else. Eve had seen a particularly tempting apple in a high tree in the middle of the garden. She was about to climb the tree to get it, when Shrewdy dropped in for a friendly visit.

"Isn't that the tree you must **not** eat from?" asked Shrewdy.

"I think so, but it looks so good!" Eve responded. "I think I'll get it and take a bite. Maybe Adam would like to share it."

Adam had fallen asleep. As usual, after lunch. So she climbed the tree and picked the apple.

"Go ahead and eat it," said Shrewdy. "To eat a beautiful apple like that can only be to your advantage."

She took a huge bite of the juicy apple. She licked a bit of the juice off her lips and and smiled. "It is good!" she told Shrewdy.

But she got so busy with her conversation with the snake that she dropped her apple. When she looked around, she saw Adam had awakened. He was about to take a large bite right out of the middle.

Eve was so mad. She hadn't even offered it to him yet. She accused Adam of stealing her apple.

Adam accused her of eating fruit she had no right to keep to herself.

Eve said it wasn't her fault, and blamed Shrewdy for the mess. He was so surprised by being blamed that it did not occur to him to apply for legal aid.

It was all silly, but the fact is that Adam and Eve had fallen out of love, and from that moment everything went wrong. As they didn't want to admit their "Fall" from love, they blamed each other. Adam became very bossy and Eve became very nasty.

One day Adam pointed rudely at Eve and said, "You're only an afterthought. God took one of my ribs to make you just for my benefit in case I got lonely or wanted someone to do jobs for me that the animals couldn't manage."

Eve was deeply hurt. She lashed back, "That one about the rib is one of your male jokes. Everyone knows that God created us in God's own image: male and female together."

Shrewdy thought he'd get in on the act so he said, "I expect God made Eve after Adam because She saw what mistakes She had made in creating Adam, and She wanted to correct them." But nobody paid any attention.

Adam and Eve continued to quarrel. They forgot to look at the blue sky and the wonderful world around them. They forgot to smell the flowers. Paradise was still there, but they could no longer see it or enjoy it.

Adam made himself a bow and arrow to go hunting. The animals began to fear for their lives. They were afraid of Adam, and they were afraid of each other. Adam persuaded Eve to cook and eat the animals as meat. He wouldn't give up hunting.

Shrewdy crawled away into the long grass and pretended to be a stick.

The animals could not understand what had happened to

them. Nor could Adam or Eve or Shrewdy. Why had this happened? No one knew. After all, hadn't Adam personally named all the animals? Was Eve annoyed at being left out of that process?

Eventually, Adam invented his own explanation. He said it was because of a god who was a mean tempered old man with a long white beard and bushy eyebrows sitting on a cloud, who was as bossy and unreasonable as he was himself.

When God saw what was happening, She wept, because She wanted her creation to be filled with love, joy, and peace. But the love between Adam and Eve had soured. They no longer saw Creation as a garden to be tended, but as their property to plunder and exploit as they wished. When God looked deeply into the heart of Adam and Eve, She saw there still lay the desire to love and be loved. In time, new life would be born from their desire.

But in the meantime, God thought, maybe they would get along better somewhere outside of Paradise. They couldn't hear the streams singing anyway. They couldn't see the flowers bending and smiling. So what was the point in their being there? Let them try their luck elsewhere.

So out they went.

Adam and Eve wandered out to the plains and camped in a cave. Since they had fallen out of love, they couldn't communicate with each other. So Adam invented a way of writing in pictures so he could pass on his version of their story in Paradise. He insisted that Eve must not learn his writing. So Eve wrote her own version of their story. She remembered the lion and the lamb playing together, so she drew that.

Adam was very angry. He destroyed what she had drawn, and drew the lion roaring at a frightened lamb. Adam was stubborn. So he continued to draw his god as an old man with a long beard, sitting on a cloud.

And that is why, to this day, people tell the Creation story mainly from Adam's point of view.

Adapted from a story by Phoebe Willetts, "Eve, Adam, and Sneaky the Snake," in *Meet Mrs. Moses*. Gooday Publishers, 1992.

Women of the Greek Scriptures

Elizabeth and Mary

Luke 1

Best friends

One of the strongest stories of solidarity between women is that of Elizabeth and Mary. Here the old and young women meet, the barren one who experiences the embarrassment of bearing a child in "old age" and the unmarried girl who is pregnant and experiences the ambiguity and shame connected with that situation.

For both of them, the deep joy and anticipation of the future is greater than the difficult circumstances. There is no hint of one being jealous of the other. In fact they unite spontaneously in their joy, which results in Mary's song known as the *Magnificat*, (Luke 1:46–56) that links God's mercy with justice between people.

The *Magnificat* is not simply a song about motherhood or the self-realization of women, but one that proclaims the liberating justice and power of God to all who are oppressed. It is precisely the difficult circumstances of her own pregnancy that make Mary sensitive to the liberating work of the Holy Spirit, and prompts the song of praise that turns conventional values topsy turvy. In the Catholic tradition in Latin America, Mary has often been used to keep women submissive. But in Luke, there is another Mary – a robust, explosive woman who asks pointed questions of Gabriel before she assumes her role in bearing the Messiah and announcing justice.

Barren Elizabeth had prayed, petitioned, and bargained with God for a child. She had fasted, tithed, kept the Sabbath, and observed Passover. She was "righteous"(Luke 1:6). She had learned to live with unanswered prayer. Then Zechariah's prayer is answered (1:13) and Elizabeth has to learn to live instead with an answered prayer. She is now pregnant with the one who will prepare the way for the Messiah (1:14–17). For five months she broods, perhaps feeling some fear and bewilderment. She has no other woman to talk to.

Mary, the poor young unmarried one (1:28), wonders how her pregnancy could possibly be? Who would believe her even if she did tell them? Would Joseph? Would Elizabeth? Just as pregnant women today seek out other pregnant women, so Mary sought out Elizabeth (1:39) who greeted her with, "Blessed are you among women and blessed is the fruit of your womb!" Solidarity at its best.

They visited for three months. What did they talk about? The changes in their bodies? The future? Their dreams? Fears of Mary's unsupported pregnancy and Elizabeth's "late" one? The suffering of people and the unjust society in need of transformation? Justice for the poor? The passion of a pregnant woman to make the world better for her child? How they would bear their "special" children and nurture them to work for justice? How would they be willing partners in the process of liberation?

Did Mary, the younger one, help Elizabeth with the chores to lighten her burden in those last drawn-out three months? This story is an imaginative reconstruction of their meeting, and of their solidarity with each other.

For further reading

Robins Wendy S. and Musimbi R. Kanyoro. *Speaking for Ourselves*. WCC, Geneva, 1990, p. 64 ff.

Weems, Renita J. *Just a Sister Away*. Lura Media, CA, 1988.

Best friends

Pregnant Mary knew for sure
that God will feed the hungry poor.
It made Elizabeth's day to say
today the rich go empty away.

Elizabeth had a baby in her womb. She was so happy she could burst!

Mary had a baby in her womb. She was so happy she could burst!

Mary went to visit her cousin Elizabeth in the city of Judah. When Elizabeth heard Mary's voice, her baby leaped for joy in her womb. Elizabeth could see the outlines of the small feet moving underneath her skin. It felt as if the baby was doing somersaults.

Elizabeth was so excited. "Why am I so blessed to have this visit from you?" she asked.

"Oh cousin, I'm so happy I could burst. I have a baby in my womb just as you do."

"How did you know?" asked Elizabeth.

"The angel Gabriel visited me. I was scared because the greeting was 'God is with you.' With **me**, a poor young girl! But Gabriel said that God loves me dearly and that I would soon have a baby in my womb and should call the baby Jesus. This baby will be a very important person. He will be in the royal line of David."

"Did you believe Gabriel?" asked Elizabeth.

"Well, I was really troubled at first. I wondered what kind of greeting it was to say 'God is with you.' And I did ask some questions. Like 'How can this be?'"

"And then?"

"And then the angel said it would happen just as announced. I'm so happy I could burst. Gabriel told me that you've had a baby in your womb for six months. I thought you were too old to have a baby. So I came right away to find out if Gabriel's promise to you is true. If it is, then probably the promise to me is true as well."

"It's true, Mary. It's true! I was so surprised," exclaimed Elizabeth, "like you. I thought I was too old to have a baby. But we **can** trust God's promises. And I'm so happy I could burst."

"What happened?" Mary asked.

"My husband Zechariah was praying at the temple one day. In a vision he had, an angel of God – the same Gabriel who came to you – told him that soon I would be having a baby son. We are to call him John."

"Did Zechariah believe what the angel told him in the vision?"

"No, he didn't. Not at first, anyway. He didn't see how it could happen after all these years. And so the angel said that my husband Zechariah would not be able to speak until the baby was born."

"And then what happened?" asked Mary.

"Just as the angel said," said Elizabeth. "I'm so happy I could burst. It's good to have you to talk to because my house is usually as quiet as a tomb. What with Zechariah not saying anything. But Mary, how long can you stay?"

"Three months, Elizabeth. Three whole months. By then your baby son will be born. I want to help you prepare the clothes, the cradle, everything. I'm so happy I could burst."

"Wonderful, Mary. It's the best time in our lives. There's so much we have to talk about. Let's start before our happiness makes us both burst!"

The Magnificat

A contemporary reflection by Dorothee Soelle

It is written that Mary said
he hath showed strength with his arm
he hath scattered the proud
he hath put down the mighty from their seats
and exalted them of low degree.

Today we express that differently
we shall dispossess our owners and we shall laugh
at those who claim to understand feminine nature
the rule of males over females will end
objects will become subjects
they will achieve their own better right.

It is written that Mary said
he hath filled the hungry with good things
and the rich he hath sent empty away.
He hath holpen his servant Israel
in remembrance of his mercy.

Today we express that differently.
Women will go to the moon and sit in parliaments
their desire for self-determination will be fulfilled
the craving for power will go unheeded
their fears will be unnecessary
and exploitation will come to an end.

—Dorothee Soelle

Dreams

Matthew 27:19

The man with kind eyes

Read Matthew chapters 27 and 28 to prepare for this story. Jesus had entered Jerusalem on Palm Sunday, greeted by crowds waving palms.

Recently, it has been discovered that, on some coins, the image of palms had been overlaid on the image of Caesar. Palms apparently were a symbol of resistance to Rome, among some parties of the Jews. Thus it is possible that, to the paranoid mind of a governor like Pontius Pilate, the identification of Jesus with palms would have suggested that Jesus was some kind of an upstart, a rebel, a potential political threat.

At the point of this reading, Jesus had already been tried by Caiaphas and the priests. They had accused him of blasphemy, and concluded that he deserved death. They turned him over to Pontius Pilate. Pilate's first question, "Are you the King of the Jews?" implies that Pilate suspected him of political motives. However, once he had interrogated Jesus, Pilate "wondered greatly" (verse 14). He was not entirely convinced that Jesus deserved death (verse 18). The note from his wife must have further unsettled him.

Finally, he washed his hands of the whole affair, released the thief Barabbas, and ordered Jesus crucified.

Was his conscience stirred by the note his wife sent him? Did he drop his eyes when confronted by Jesus' forthright gaze? His feeble response, washing his hands, speaks more of relief at getting out of the whole affair without further blame or rioting than of his own integrity. He had, after all, his own position to protect.

Pilate's wife wrote the note because, in my interpretation of her dream, Jesus had saved both her son and her unborn baby from the howling mob. In her eyes, he was "righteous" because he put children first.

The man with kind eyes

Dreams can take you over the rainbow.
Dreams can make you as free as the sea.
Of all the many dreams I know
The best ones make me truly me.

"Mommy, Mommy," my son cried.

"What is it, child?" I asked urgently as I came into Cassius' room. I gathered him into my arms and hugged and rocked him.

"I had a nightmare, Mommy. A horrible one. There were big eyes all around, chasing me."

"There, there, dear," I said, patting him. "Tell me all about it."

"And there were men without eyes, just big hollows where their eyes should have been. They were chasing me down the street, under a bridge, and they came right into my bedroom. It was horrible. I was so scared." He was trembling.

"But you know it was only a dream, don't you?" I comforted him.

"I dreamed about that parade that was in Jerusalem a few days ago," he poured out a stream of words. "I was with my friends. We were laughing and shouting, breaking off palm branches like the other kids. But suddenly those angry men without eyes came chasing me. They screamed at me without making any noise. Their mouths were open and cruel, but I couldn't hear any sound from them.

"But that man who was riding on a donkey in the parade stopped, and got down from his donkey. He came and hugged me and all the eyeless men ran away. I think it was the same man I heard the servants talking about. The man who is in court with Daddy right now. He saved me, Mommy. He saved me. His eyes were so kind."

He was still trembling with fright, but calming down. After a while, I kissed him goodnight and he fell asleep, quietly and peacefully.

It was so hot. Jerusalem can be miserable at this time of year. The baby in my womb kicked and turned. I could hear crowds yelling outside the palace. It's probably the usual crop of angry young men who want to free their country from Rome. They were all out at the parade the other day, waving their palm branches defiantly against Rome. It was some Jewish festival or other – something about them celebrating the anniversary of their god parting the seas.

I don't know why we had to come to this god-forsaken land, this backwater, where we have to stave off riots by the skin of our teeth. And me expecting a baby. It's no time and no place to bring a child into the world.

I lay in bed, tossing and thinking, unable to sleep in the humid night.

Finally I fell into a troubled sleep. I didn't think I had slept a wink, but I must have, because I had a dream. It was horrible. In my dream, the crowds were rioting. I was in the middle of it, holding Cassius by the hand. My servants, my bodyguards, were nowhere around. We were shoved; I was afraid of being trampled. We were chased by men without eyes, just big hollows where their eyes should have been. They were wild and angry men, shouting at us without making a sound. The most horrifying thing was that the baby I'm expecting was in the dream – but without eyes. The hands of the angry men reached out to grab my newborn baby.

Then that man on the donkey – the one who rode into Jerusalem a few days ago, the one who was in Cassius' dream – came into my dream too. He had the kindest eyes I've ever seen. He reached out and hugged Cassius. Then he cradled my baby in his arms, and suddenly my baby had sparkling eyes. There were four or five women walking with him. They smiled at all the children along the way, including my Cassius. They all had eyes, very kind eyes. Some were full of sadness, but full of love too.

And the angry eyeless men just faded away.

I woke up gasping and sweating, the dream was so real.

My husband Pontius was already in court when I woke up. I knew he had to deal with the case of that man on the donkey. His name was Jesus, I think. He had gotten on the wrong side of the local authorities somehow. They got hold of him yesterday. They sentenced him to death in one of their kangaroo courts – as if they had any right to hold court at all.

Now Pontius has to sort it out.

Immediately, I sent my servant girl over with a note. "Don't have anything to do with that good man," I wrote. "Leave him alone. I went through agonies dreaming about him last night."

I wonder what Pontius will do when he reads my note. My husband Pontius is very powerful, but he's not always very honorable. He can be callous. When the steady eyes of that man on the donkey meet his, which one will look away?

When those kind and steady eyes look into my husband's eyes, will they see big hollows where his eyes should have been?

Nancy's scary dream

Based on Matthew 27:19

One morning Nancy was telling her mother about the dream she'd had the night before.

"It was the strangest dream! And it was scary. I was on a roller coaster, eating ice cream with my best friend, when suddenly a dinosaur plucked me off, sat me on his back, trotted off, and dropped me into Lake Superior. It was February so it was freezing cold. I had a terrible time swimming and almost drowned. I was scared. But finally, sputtering and sneezing, I reached the other side of the lake. When I landed, a girl whose skin was green with yellow polka dots gave me a paintbrush and told me to climb to the top of the roof of this house to paint it. It was a very steep roof, and a rickety old house, and I knew I shouldn't climb up without someone standing by. But I did anyway. I was half way up when – boom! Down I came. And that's when I woke up – on the floor beside my bed."

Her mother laughed. "Well, Nancy, you remember you wanted to go swimming in early May at the lake and I told you you couldn't – it was just too cold. And you're only seven years old, you know – not old enough yet to dive off the high board. Maybe your dream was a warning."

Nancy told her Sunday school teacher her scary dream.

In turn, her teacher told her an Easter Bible story about a scary dream. It was a warning too!

"When the people were deciding whether to put Jesus to death or not," the teacher said, "the man in charge was named Pilate. At the big feast time, it was the custom to set free for the crowd, any prisoner whom they wanted. There was a really rotten man in prison. Barabbas, he was called. Pilate kind of liked Jesus. He thought if he gave the crowd a choice between rotten Barabbas and Jesus, they might choose to set Jesus free. Pilate thought that Jesus' enemies just wanted him out of the way because they were jealous of his good works and his popularity with the crowds. So why wouldn't the crowd choose Jesus? Then Pilate wouldn't have to make the decision himself.

"Besides, Pilate's wife had a dream about Jesus! Her dream was so strong that she sent a message to Pilate. It said, 'Don't have anything to do with harming that good man! I went through agonies dreaming about him last night.'

"But Pilate didn't pay attention to his wife's dream. When he offered the crowd the choice of whom they wanted set free, they cried, 'Barabbas!' and they booooooed Jesus."

Nancy wondered what would have happened to Jesus if Pilate had really really listened to his wife's scary dream.

"Of course," said the teacher, "not all dreams are scary. Most are wonderful."

Then she said that next week she wanted everyone to tell about their very **best** dream. And she promised tell some of the **wonderful** dreams in the Bible.

The widow's mite

Luke 21:1–4; Mark 12:41–44

Just an old woman

This tale imaginatively marries two separate gospel stories. One is of the widow who put her last two coins into the temple treasury ("all the living that she had"). The other is the story of Jesus' birth when, in Bethlehem, the inn was full and Joseph and Mary were turned away.

Widows were at the very bottom of the social, economic heap. With no man to support them or relate to them, they were insignificant nobodies. They were poor and lived on next to nothing. Yet here is a widow giving "all her living" generously, to support the work of the temple.

Bill Hendry, the author of this story, takes a leap of the imagination. He wonders, "Suppose this widow had been present at Jesus' birth. What might she have been thinking?"

We assume that she had never forgotten the night of Jesus' birth, and how she had been instrumental in making sure the stable was warm and clean. No doubt she had followed his life story as he grew to manhood. She would have a special place in her heart for his teachings, and that became clear when she contributed her two copper coins.

Being a widow, she was used to staying in the background. Not surprisingly, then, she didn't identify herself to Jesus.

The poignancy of the story lies in just that fact. She, of all people, would be most welcomed by Jesus. But she would never thrust herself into his attention.

Just an old woman

by Rev. William Hendry, Kingston, Ontario

I'm just a poor widow
who witnessed his birth,
But years and years later
I saw his true worth.

Jesus stood at the steps of the treasury...

I don't know if he saw me or knew me...but I have known him for a long time.

My name is Deborah. I was there when he was born, 30 years ago. I was 14 then...

I'm 44 now – not really old, but old for my days. My husband died several years ago and I have no family. It has been difficult to keep myself fed and clothed. I care for the babies of the young women I know, and they give me a little money to buy food at the market. I come regularly to the market and to the temple as well. When I've saved a coin or two, I put them in the temple treasury and give thanks to God.

People come from all over to make their gifts. I felt so small with what I had to give, just two small coins.

When I was 14, I used to help my dad the innkeeper. I put clean linen on the beds, washed dishes, and tended the animals in the stable. I especially liked the camels. Camels are gentle and really big. When they lie down for the night you can rub their heads and faces and they just close their eyes. They make a purring sound like kittens.

I remember that year. The emperor of Rome, Caesar Augustus, had declared that a census would be taken. All over our land, people were returning to their home towns to be counted. Oh, it was busy. I had to run to keep up with the work – watering and feeding the camels, making the beds, and helping Dad in the kitchen.

I remember the young couple coming to Bethlehem to our inn. We were filled up. She was about to have a child and she was very tired. I guess it had been a long journey for them. Dad asked some of the other guests if they would give up their rooms, but they had come great distances too, and no one wanted to. Dad had even rented out our own rooms. We slept in the kitchen those nights.

This young woman and her husband were really sad. The wind had started to blow and it was dark.

"They can stay in the stable. I'll go out and take some straw and put it around the edge of that large stall, to keep the wind out," I blurted.

My dad hesitated.

"And they can have the blanket I have in the kitchen. What do you think, Dad? Is it all right? It'll only take me a few minutes to make things ready," I pleaded.

Before Dad could say no I was off making the stable clean and warm.

The young woman and her husband had just got settled in when she went into labor. I had helped last year when my aunt gave birth to her daughter, so I wasn't as frightened as I had been the first time. I remember thinking how quiet it was at first. I couldn't hear the wind. The camels were down – all the people inside the inn full to overflowing – but there was no sound until the birthing started. Her breathing became heavier and louder as she labored to bear her child. She began to sweat. Her hands squeezed mine tightly. Her moans were echoed by the noise the barn animals started to make as if in sympathy – the bleating of the lambs and the braying of the donkeys. A final push and out came a little head, wispy with very dark hair.

It was a boy! I helped to bathe him and hand him to his mother. She named him Jesus.

It's hard to believe – here he stood at the foot of the steps today, watching. I wonder if he noticed me. I wonder if it would be all right if I told him I was there the night he was born.

No, I'd better not. I'm just an old widow.

From a workshop in storytelling at Queen's Theological College, Kingston, Ontario

Jesus and the children

Matthew 18:1–6 and 10–14; Matthew 19:13–15;
Mark 10:13–16; Luke 18:15–17

Even the ones with runny noses

Mark gives the fullest treatment of this well-known story. However, there are variations in Matthew 17:24 and Matthew 18 that are worth looking at. In particular, Matthew 17 tells of a "magic trick" that I have incorporated into this story, and Matthew 18 gives some background on what Jesus really felt about children. To receive the kingdom of God "as a child" is to give up power over others. It is to adopt a stance of humility (18:4) and not to dominate others.

That is a hard teaching for many Christians in the Western world who have been taught that we are the world's benefactors and teachers. We have yet to adopt the attitude of a child, the attitude that expects to learn from those we refer to (often with pity) as the "Third World" – by which we mean the poor, the undesirable, the marginal... Occasionally, we talk about the "Third World" in our midst: the Native people, the street people, the prostitutes... It is difficult for us to abandon the attitude that "we know best."

In the Bible, the laying on of hands signified a life-long, irreversible blessing for the one on whom it was bestowed. This blessing was believed to be incredibly powerful. Isaac gave such a blessing to Jacob. Later, in Genesis 48, Jacob in turn lays hands on his grandchildren Ephraim and Mannaseh. But because he crossed his hands as he did it, he gave the major blessing to the younger child, Ephraim, who would normally be considered insignificant. This caused Joseph, the boys' father and Jacob's favorite son, great discomfort. He thought the major blessing should have gone to the supposedly more important firstborn grandson, Mannaseh.

In the stories of Jesus and the children, the gospels record a similar reversal of expectations. Jesus taking the children in his arms, blessing them, and laying his hands upon them, is the same kind of irreversible, powerful blessing of those who appeared to be less deserving, less significant – the little children! It is as if he's doing a dramatized illustration of his entire message by this action. He says, in effect, be as humble and as expectant as little children, all who wish to enter the kingdom.

Even the ones with runny noses

Tender and bright, refusing to fight –
That's what little boys are made of.
Subversive and strong, the whole day long –
That's what little girls are made of.

It was a bright beautiful day. White cotton-puff clouds were scudding across the blue sky, pushed by a gentle breeze off the lake.

My mom and I were going to the hills outside the village to meet a famous teacher. His name was Jesus. Mom wanted him to heal my little brother David. David was hopelessly sick most of the time. It made my mom sad. But Jesus was famous for his healing touch.

We'd also heard how he had fed a huge crowd out on the hills one day. I guess we hoped the same thing might happen this time. We were hungry most of the time. I often wished I could magically find some bread and fish on our doorstep, but it never happened. We didn't have much lunch to take with us, because there were nine of us kids. Mom said we had too many mouths to feed.

Of course, we were late getting started. Too many things to look after, Mom said, shaking her head. She shakes her head a lot these days. I put on my only tunic, even if it did have a tear in it. Mom tried to get us looking clean and neat, but I didn't have time to wash my face and hands. But I didn't think anyone would notice. Besides, I'd have had to fetch water to do it.

When we arrived, there was this man sitting on a rock telling stories. We kids started to amuse ourselves, since we didn't see any food around. My brother Joel set to work building a tower of stones. There were lots of stones around. Matthew threw some of the stones at the birds nesting in the nearby trees. Abe discovered an ant hill, and was picking up ants and squishing them between his fingers. I found some of my friends, and we started a game of hide and seek.

A few of the men standing around beside the famous teacher came to us. "Shhhhhh!" they hissed. "Can't you see the teacher is speaking?"

Of course we could see that he was speaking. But he wasn't speaking to **us.** So we quieted down for a bit. But soon the game got noisy again.

"Shhhhhh!" they hissed again. "Stop this noise and racing around. Or go away home!"

My friends and I huddled in a circle, sitting on the ground. I didn't like the men who told us to keep quiet. "Who do they think they are?" I grumbled to my friends. "Do they think they own this hill?"

"Shhhhhhh!" the men hissed for a third time. "Go away! Play somewhere else! You're disturbing the teacher." And they waved their arms, shooing us away from the teacher.

My mom was carrying David in her arms. She wanted to get close enough to Jesus so he could touch my brother. But there was quite a crowd, and she wasn't the only mother trying to get close to him. I could hear her whispering to the crowd of men, closest to the teacher, trying to get through.

"Sshhhhh!" hissed the men again, this time to the mothers. "Can't you see he's busy?"

By this time, the teacher had noticed what was going on.

"Let the children come to me if their mothers wish it," he said. "Don't shoo them away. For the little people are the most important people to me."

Then he stood up, and motioned to the hissing men to make a path to him and a space around him, and he signaled to the mothers to bring their children up to him. My mom was right there. He sat down on the rock again, and cradled David in his arms, not even noticing David's runny nose or grungy clothes. Mom had Abe with her, and Jesus hugged him with his left arm, not even noticing Abe's hands that were filthy with mud and crushed ants.

"I think your voices are one of God's favorite sounds," he said to my friends and me. We had stopped making noises for a minute to watch him.

Then he turned to the mothers. "Unless you become like little children, you cannot be part of my company," he announced. "A little child is the greatest and most precious gift to me," he went on, with his face smiling and his hands on the heads of David and Abe. "God does not want any one of these little people hurt or sick."

By now David's nose was running all over the place. But the man didn't notice, or he didn't care. He just hugged him, and David's face lit up.

I didn't see any bread and fish suddenly appearing. But what I did see was Mom's face. It was as bright and fresh as the breeze that sent the clouds scudding along in the blue sky. She was smiling and full of hope for the first time I could remember.